Praise for *Wake Up Now*

"This book is one of the most concise guides to spiritual awakening I have read. Both profound and practical, it guides the reader through the intricacies of awakening as only someone who has walked the walk themselves can do. The clarity and compassion this book offers the sincere spiritual seeker is both rare and welcome."

—Adyashanti, author of *The Impact of Awakening* and *Emptiness Dancing*

"Many books talk about spiritual awakening, but *Wake Up Now* breaks new ground by providing a detailed road map to the complete awakening process. Profound yet accessible, precise yet jargon-free, this wise book leads you step-by-step on the direct path home to your radiant natural state, your innermost true self."

—Lama Surya Das, author of *Awakening the Buddha Within*

"Communicating nondual wisdom is a high art—requiring a precise and evocative use of language, as well as a profound understanding of paradox. In *Wake Up Now*, Stephan Bodian more than manages both of these challenges and provides the fortunate reader with a doorway into the real but ineffable possibilities inherent in this very moment."

—Stephen Cope, director of the Kripalu Institute for Extraordinary Living and author of *Yoga and the Quest for the True Self*

"Read Stephan Bodian's *Wake Up Now* to do just that. It cuts through everything!"

—David Chadwick, author of *Crooked Cucumber: The Life and Zen Teaching of Shunryu Suzuki*

"Stephan Bodian masterfully presents enlightenment not as a state to be achieved, but as our underlying condition that is already present, only awaiting recognition. This is a must read for all who sincerely desire a direct pointer to absolute truth and to living the awakened life."

—Richard Miller, Ph.D., cofounder of the International Association of Yoga Therapy and author of *Yoga Nidra: The Meditative Heart of Yoga*

"Stephan gently takes you by the hand and guides you home through the spiritual maze to your innate awakened essence, awareness itself. *Wake Up Now* is an extraordinarily user-friendly, radiant gem."

—Leonard Laskow, M.D., author of *Healing with Love*

"*Wake Up Now* is a timely book. Not only does it invite the reader to step out of the mind into our natural state, but it also paints the possibility of fully embodying that awakening in day-to-day life. Stephan Bodian is one of a growing breed of 'translucent' writers and teachers who point us to a new vision of the possibilities of being human."

—Arjuna Ardagh, author of *The Translucent Revolution*

WAKE UP
NOW

WAKE UP
NOW

·

A GUIDE *to the* JOURNEY
of SPIRITUAL AWAKENING

STEPHAN BODIAN

New York   Chicago   San Francisco   Lisbon   London   Madrid   Mexico City
Milan   New Delhi   San Juan   Seoul   Singapore   Sydney   Toronto

Library of Congress Cataloging-in-Publication Data

Bodian, Stephan.
    Wake up now : a guide to the journey of spiritual awakening / Stephan
Bodian.
        p.   cm.
    Includes index.
    ISBN 13: 978-0-07-149428-1 (alk. paper)
    ISBN 10: 0-07-149428-6 (alk. paper)
    1. Spirituality.   2. Spiritual biography.   I. Title.

    BL624.B61622   2008
    204'.4—dc22   2007031608

1 2 3 4 5 6 7 8 9 10 11 12 13 14 15 16 17 18 19   FGR/FGR   0 9 8 7

ISBN   978-0-07-149428-1
MHID   0-07-149428-6

Interior design by designforbooks.com

McGraw-Hill books are available at special quantity discounts to use as premiums
and sales promotions, or for use in corporate training programs. For more
information, please write to the Director of Special Sales, Professional Publishing,
McGraw-Hill, Two Penn Plaza, New York, NY 10121-2298. Or contact your local
bookstore.

This book is printed on acid-free paper.

To Consciousness,
the silent source and essence of all.

And to you, dear reader:
May this book illuminate your journey of awakening.

CONTENTS

ACKNOWLEDGMENTS

Needless to say, a book of this kind is the fruition of count-less insights and experiences, many of them precipitated or inspired by the kind support and compassionate presence of others. As the words poured forth and appeared on the page, it was clear that this person here is merely an instrument of a more universal movement of truth.

First, I offer heartfelt thanks to my many friends and colleagues, for the love and wisdom we've shared over the years; to my students and clients, who kept asking questions and eliciting clarification; and to my friend and Dharma brother John Prendergast, who read the manuscript care-fully and offered invaluable suggestions and feedback.

Thanks also to the folks who made possible the publica-tion of this book: my agent, Bill Gladstone, who believed in the proposal and found it a good home; and my editors at McGraw-Hill, Doug Corcoran and Sarah Pelz, for their enthusiastic support at every stage of the process.

Finally, I offer deep bows of appreciation to my teachers, without whose dedication and compassion this book would never have been written: Shunryu Suzuki Roshi; Kobun Chino Otogawa Roshi; Taizan Maezumi Roshi; Tsoknyi Rinpoche; and, especially, Jean Klein and Adyashanti. My gratitude for their generosity and their commitment to truth knows no bounds.

INTRODUCTION

Like numerous other authors of spiritual guides, I was motivated to write this book by the complexities and confusion
I experienced on my own spiritual journey. Despite all the
guidance I received through many years of study and practice in several established traditions, I often found myself
wandering alone in uncharted terrain as I navigated my way
among the various openings, glimpses, obstacles, and challenges I encountered.

In the Zen tradition, where I practiced as a monk for
more than a decade, awakening to true self, or "Buddha
nature," was the elusive goal of the spiritual path, the reason
we sat for long, arduous hours facing a wall and following
our breath or wrestling with one of the hundreds of koans,
or riddles, in the Zen canon. But the nature of this awakening, or *kensho*, was rarely explained or described in detail.
Indeed, such descriptions were scrupulously avoided to
prevent us from fabricating some false, imitation awakening
based on what we had heard. We were encouraged to read
stories depicting the enlightenment experiences of the great
masters of the past. But inevitably the awakening—which
was generally precipitated by an unexpected event, like a
pebble striking bamboo or a sudden blow from the teacher's

staff—was instantaneous and apparently complete, and its substance, the realization the practitioner awakened to, was described in deliberately elliptical and poetic language to prevent any neophyte from prematurely deciphering the code. As a result, I was left to stumble my way toward enlightenment on my own, with frequent visits to the roshi to assess my progress and validate any authentic insights.

After ten years of this regime, I left the monastery and put aside my robes because I concluded that I wasn't getting any closer to the realization I so earnestly sought; the advice of my teachers—essentially to meditate longer and "sit harder"—no longer resonated and proved fruitless in practice. Sure, I had had a few fleeting glimpses of a profound stillness and silence beneath the activity and clamor of life— brief moments, once while riding my motorcycle, another while sitting by a mountain stream, when time seemed to stand still in the luminosity of the eternal Now. After one of these experiences, a lifetime of anxiety lifted and did not return for several weeks. But I knew that I hadn't reached the summit of the mountain, and my appraisal was echoed by my Zen teacher, who would approve my presentations of the koans, then periodically pause, peer at me over his reading glasses, and say with some affection, "Not quite clear."

For the next few years, I dabbled in other forms of Buddhist practice, including Vipassana and Tibetan Vajrayana, before happening inadvertently on a master of the Indian tradition known as Advaita ("nondual") Vedanta. Instead of encouraging his students to meditate in order to achieve enlightenment, as I had been accustomed to do, he taught that our always already awakened true nature was our birth-right, our inherent condition, our natural state, which we merely needed to recognize, without effort or striving, in a moment out of time. After so many years of just such effort and striving, I found his words to be a tremendous relief—and actually quite familiar, since they echoed the teachings of the early Zen masters who were so revered (though not so often followed in practice) in the Buddhist tradition.

Under this teacher's guidance, I had a profound and unmistakable awakening to the living truth of who I really am. But instead of the awakening being complete and irreversible, as I had expected, for days I found myself oscillating between vast spaciousness and peace and overwhelming fear bordering on panic. I felt as if the bottom had dropped out of my familiar, albeit unsatisfactory, life, and I had no place to land—and I experienced this groundlessness as alternately exhilarating and terrifying.

Over time, the awakening receded into the background of my awareness, but whenever it reasserted itself, I would feel a renewed rush of anxiety. I knew I had experienced a genuine, profound, life-altering recognition of the reality that underlies all appearance, yet I couldn't figure out why I was still so afraid so much of the time. Had I done something wrong? Was I mistaken in my assessment? Was the awakening misguided or incomplete in some way? These questions haunted me in my years with this teacher, and instead of putting an end to my search, my experience just fueled further doubts about my spiritual maturity—and my relative sanity. From my reading and the teachings I'd received, I had come to believe that true awakening should be complete and irreversible. Then why did I seem to keep forgetting who I was and lapsing back into identification with the me, the "small self"?

Unfortunately, I never felt comfortable asking these questions of my teacher, perhaps because he seemed reluctant to address such psychological issues and perhaps also because I wanted to appear more confident of my understanding than I actually was. Besides, in his presence such questions inevitably dropped away, my fears evaporated, my mind quieted down, and I joined him in the profound stillness and silence that he embodied and transmitted.

Eventually, I met a woman who helped me assuage my doubts because her journey had been similar to mine. After a sudden, explosive awakening to the illusory nature of the separate self, she spent years in constant fear before opening to an even deeper realization in which all fear dropped away. Trained as a psychologist, she had the sophistication necessary to bridge the two worlds and say, with the conviction and authority born of personal experience, that fear by no means undermines the validity of awakening, but is rather just another arising among many in the vastness of who we are. This subtle shift in perception allowed me to reframe my fear, and it gradually began losing its hold over me. Finally, some years later, soon after the death of my Advaita master of ten years, I met the teacher who confirmed and helped me clarify and deepen my realization and ultimately asked me to teach.

THE DIRECT APPROACH TO AWAKENING

In my own years as a spiritual teacher and psychotherapist, I've discovered that my circuitous journey was by no means unique. Many people are drawn to spiritual awakening but have difficulty locating teachings or teachers that speak directly to their experience in language they can understand. Some have discovered the possibility of waking up and seek clear guidance that points them toward the awakening experience without religious jargon or dogma. Others awaken suddenly and unexpectedly to a reality they don't have the conceptual framework to handle or have experiences along the way that don't fit the descriptions in traditional texts. They may have no interest in or contact with Buddhism or Hinduism, the religions most often associated with spiritual awakening, and therefore have no access to guidance in making sense of their experiences. Or they may be practitioners within these traditions but find that their teachers can't help because the teachers haven't had the same experiences themselves.

One student of mine, for example, had practiced Transcendental Meditation for many years and had come to expect that spiritual awakening would take the form of "cosmic consciousness" as described by the founder of that technique. Instead, she had a profound experience of no-self that felt more like a bad dream or psychotic break than a fortuitous cosmic event because she didn't have a teacher who could guide her through it. Another student, who had been told by his Tibetan Buddhist teachers that enlightenment took lifetimes to achieve, came to me to help him come to terms with the powerful shift in identity he had experienced one day while walking in the woods.

Other people awaken without any prior preparation or even any interest in spiritual matters. They don't have access to the guidelines and pointers found in traditional spiritual texts, and even if they did, they wouldn't have the language or the philosophical context to interpret what they read. Still others, longtime spiritual seekers, have no problem identifying their awakening as authentic, but they find themselves surprised and confused when the "awakeness" they've spent so long pursuing keeps wavering or fading, and their life seems to become even more challenging and tumultuous, rather than more reliably peaceful and joyful, as they were led to expect.

I've written this book for seekers like these who are looking for direct guidance in plain language on the often prolonged and complex journey of spiritual awakening. If you aspire to awaken or have already experienced an initial awakening, then this book is definitely intended for you. As I've discovered, awakening doesn't belong to one teaching or tradition, and in any case, once you wake up, you actually awaken out of traditional frameworks. After all, if you're awakening to your true nature, the one you've always already been deep down inside, how could one tradition or approach have a monopoly on it? This precious spiritual nature has always belonged to you, and, like one version of the proverbial prodigal son, you're merely discovering the diamond that's been hidden in your pocket all along.

In fact, more and more people appear to be awakening to their inherent spiritual nature, whether or not they've been practicing meditation or some other prescribed technique. Perhaps it's just our technological times, when experiences are shared so much more globally through cell phones, e-mails, websites, and blogs, but awakening seems to have shed the garments of religion and revealed itself for what it is—a universal human experience available to everyone right here and now. Despite what you may have been led to believe, enlightenment is your birthright, your natural state—you merely need to reclaim and learn to embody it.

In this book, I offer a direct approach to enlightenment that circumvents the elaborate rituals, practices, and teachings of traditional religions such as Buddhism and Hinduism. Instead of requiring you to pledge allegiance to certain beliefs or adhere to preestablished spiritual practices, I point directly, again and again, to the truth of who you are and invite you to resonate with the source from which the words arise, allowing it to awaken to itself inside you. Instead of helping you to construct a new and more comforting belief system, I encourage you to investigate and penetrate the many ideas and preconceptions you already hold in order to reach the living truth that lies beneath. This approach to spirituality is actually quite radical, because it goes right to the root or source from which all spirituality springs and invites you to abide there, rather than hanging out in the leaves and branches.

At the same time, this approach is definitely not "awakening lite," a quick little shortcut to enjoyable experiences that you can add to your spiritual résumé. Quite the contrary, these teachings are potent and subversive, and once received and considered, they have the power to transform your life in unexpected and possibly uncomfortable ways. They're like spiritual computer viruses with the power to wipe your hard drive clean of concepts and fill it with the clarity and wisdom of truth. Or if you prefer nature metaphors, they're like seeds that, once planted, have the potential to grow into radiant flowers that crowd out the old weeds in your yard. Whatever image resonates for you, just know that you read this book at your own peril, for you may not be able to return to your old way of seeing things again.

WHAT IS AWAKENING?

In the broadest sense, the term *awakening* is merely an evocative metaphor that's been bandied about in spiritual books for years to cover a range of experiences. Any experience can be considered an awakening if it opens you to a new, previously unrecognized dimension of being. For example, you can awaken to your sexuality, to the energy fields of the body, or to the mythic gods and goddesses of the archetypal realm.

But the awakening I'm talking about in this book is deeper, more essential, and more transformative—it's a fundamental recognition of the inherent insubstantiality or emptiness of the person you take yourself to be and a radical shift in your identity from being the suffering separate self to being the eternal witness, the limitless space or ground in which all experiences arise. In other words, you awaken *from* the dream of suffering and separation *to* the radiance and joy of your true nature. More than being merely one spiritual experience among many, this awakening (often called enlightenment) is the essential realization at the heart of the Eastern spiritual traditions of Buddhism, Hinduism, and Taoism, and it can also be found as a more subterranean current in Judaism, Christianity, and Islam—though mystics have been excommunicated, ostracized, or burned at the stake for making such pronouncements.

When you awaken, you realize that the separate person you took yourself to be is just a construct, a mental fabrication—a collection of thoughts, feelings, memories, beliefs, and stories that have been woven together by the mind into the appearance of a substantial, continuous someone with certain abiding qualities and characteristics. By freeing you from your identification with the separate self, awakening liberates you from the burdens and concerns, worries and regrets, limitations and preoccupations that the person bearing your name has accumulated over a lifetime. But this construct has extraordinary tenacity, and it generally won't give up without a prolonged struggle to stay in control.

After all, if you're like most people, you've devoted your life to enhancing, developing, improving, and promoting this apparently separate someone in order to win love, succeed, get ahead, and finally achieve more happiness and fulfillment. You're not about to give it up lightly. Besides, your family, friends, teachers, and colleagues have encouraged you in your identity because they're equally committed to their own dream of separate personhood. As a result, you live your life believing that you're just a limited character in the dream and may never realize that there's an alternative, another way to experience yourself: you can awaken out of the dream and discover that you're the dreamer, the observer, the source of the dream itself.

Then one day, you have an unexpected glimpse behind the veil of conventional reality to a mysterious perspective you never knew existed. Maybe you're driving your car along a familiar street when time seems to stand still and the shops and people lose their usual solidity and become like figures projected on a screen. Or you're walking in nature when suddenly you sense a deeper energy or radiance behind the flowers and trees. Or you're lying in bed when the boundaries of your body dissolve and you expand to include the entire universe. Such provocative experiences, though not awakening itself, open you to the possibility of seeing life in a completely new way and set you on a search for the deeper truth that lurks unrecognized behind the dream of ordinary life.

Alternatively, you may be introduced to the possibility of awakening by reading the words of the great enlightened masters and sages, who point directly to the greater reality beyond the dream and lovingly encourage you to join them in the peace and joy they've discovered there. "You're not the person you imagine yourself to be," they keep repeating, "not this limited physical body or this obsessed and worried mind, but unlimited space, unconditioned presence, the essence and spirit at the heart of life itself. Just wake up and realize it!" You don't have to go off to India or read scores of books to ignite a yearning to discover this truth. Even a single phrase or teaching can capture your attention and refuse to let you go, gradually challenging and undermining your limited view.

You may even have a complete awakening, in which the locus of your identity shifts from being the body, mind, and personality to being the eternal witness, the limitless space. Now what? What do you do if the experience begins to fade or strong feelings or old patterns intrude? What do you make of the experience, and how can you relate to it in order to nurture and deepen it?

No matter how you're ambushed or seduced by awakening, you've stumbled on a path that's been hidden from view until now—a path that's been traveled by countless people before you and continues to be traveled now by kindred spirits everywhere. In fact, it's a pathless path because it's unique to each seeker and keeps changing as the journey unfolds. Even more essentially, it isn't really a path at all, because there's nowhere to go and nothing to discover; everything you need to know and be is right here and now—indeed, it is the very here and now that you are. But until you fully understand the truth of these words, you've embarked on a journey that eventually meanders its way back home. It's the journey of awakening, the journey to free yourself from the dream of separation and wake up to who you really are—and once you've awakened, to stay that way and allow the awakeness to inform and transform you. This book is intended as a guidebook on your journey home, a road map for the pathless path.

WHAT DO YOU AWAKEN TO?

Once you penetrate the illusory nature of the separate self, you discover that what really lives this life, peers out through these eyes, thinks these thoughts, and animates these arms and legs is not the personality, which is just a lifeless construct, but being itself, which can't be located or grasped with the hands or mind but can be directly intuited or apperceived. In other words, you can know with certainty what you are, but you may not quite be able to describe how you know.

The various terms used to delineate being—*spirit, soul, true self, Buddha nature, God within*—are like so many labels pinned on empty space. Pure being can't be pinned down because it has no characteristics in itself; rather, it's the ever-present witness of all characteristics, the unchanging space in which all experiences come and go, the unmoved mover behind all activity, the limitless source of all things.

Everything you can hear, see, smell, taste, touch, feel, and think—that is, everything with qualities or characteristics—is an experience, an object of your observation, and therefore can't possibly be the you who experiences or observes. The question is, who or what is this you, this me? Even the me you've taken yourself to be, the self-image, the personality, is just a collection of characteristics and can't be the one who experiences. Spiritual awakening means waking up to the experiencer, the witness, pure being itself, the one who is eternally aware.

Words can't possibly encompass the vastness of being or pin down its mystery, but they can be used as convenient pointers, like fingers that point to the moon but have nothing to do with the moon itself. The terms and phrases used throughout this book, such as *impersonal witness, ultimate subject, timeless presence,* are not intended as concepts to add to your spiritual encyclopedia. Instead, their purpose is to short-circuit your conceptual mind and point beyond it to the place inside you that already knows what I'm talking about and can recognize and resonate with the truth of these words. If the words do their job, you'll put down this book knowing less than when you picked it up but being closer to true, nonconceptual understanding.

THE STAGES OF AWAKENING

As powerful as waking up to pure being or the impersonal witness may be, it's just the beginning of an often pro-longed journey of spiritual unfolding. Like an earthquake in consciousness, awakening moves the tectonic plates of your psyche and sends shock waves to every corner of your life, initiating a profound transformation at the core of your being. Over time, the awakening will deepen and expand as you become progressively clearer about who you really are. Along with greater clarity, you'll feel a natural movement to live in alignment with your realization. Eventually, the truth you've awakened to will become the predominant perspec-tive and force in your life, supplanting the old beliefs and stories that have informed your activities in the past.

For some people, this process of transformation happens slowly and almost imperceptibly, like gradually getting wet while walking through fog. Others may experience it as a tsunami roaring across the landscape of their lives and leav-ing nothing undisturbed in its wake. Whether you're just

ambling along on your journey or feeling as though your
world is falling apart, you can benefit from having a guide
who outlines the stages of the pathless path and reassures
you that you're actually right on track and doing just fine.

Based on my own experience and the experiences of
students and clients over the years, I've broken down the
awakening process into five overlapping stages: seeking,
awakening, deepening and clarifying, embodying, and living
the awakened life. These stages, which are explored at great
length in this book and echo traditional categories from Zen
and Tibetan Buddhism, are meant to be only loosely sequen-
tial, and most people skip around from one to another in the
course of their journey. Indeed, every person's spiritual tra-
jectory is unique, and no map can hope to chart the terrain
accurately for everyone. Ultimately, you are the path—the
path begins and ends with you. Maps are just intended
to quiet the mind so it can relax and allow the process to
unfold. Don't take them too seriously—in fact, don't take
anything in this book too seriously. If you find some insight
helpful in reassuring or orienting you, hold it lightly; if it
causes you to doubt yourself or fear the possibilities, forget
about it—you can pick it up later if it appeals to you again.

Here is a brief overview of the stages I'll be describing:

• **Seeking (Chapters 1 through 5).** Motivated by suffering, devotion, or mere curiosity, you stumble on the
possibility of awakening and begin to search for it using a
variety of means to glimpse it for yourself. In this stage, you
may learn to sit quietly, practice self-inquiry, and closely

examine the various spiritual beliefs you've accumulated over the years that may obscure your inherent wakefulness. Even after your initial awakening, you may continue seeking if you feel that your awakening is not quite clear or complete.

• **Awakening (Chapter 6).** In the aftermath of authentic, direct, nonconceptual awakening, seeking comes to an end. You've found what you've been looking for, know who you are, recognize your original face, and have discovered the priceless jewel of true nature.

• **Deepening and clarifying (Chapter 7).** In most cases, awakening continues to unfold and clarify, just as you may recognize a familiar face from afar but only gradually begin to flesh out the important details as you get closer. In particular, the recognition that you are the light of consciousness, pure awareness, the impersonal witness, gradually deepens as you realize that the witness and what is witnessed, observer and observed, subject and object, you and the objects of your experience, are inseparable. To take this even further, they are both manifestations of some deeper reality or mystery that enlivens, encompasses, and gives rise to everything.

• **Embodiment (Chapters 8 and 9).** Although you may know who you are with unshakable certainty, this realization may still have to filter down from your mind and heart into your lower energy centers. As a result, you may experience your oneness with all things and enjoy the bliss of timeless presence when you sit quietly by yourself, but you may not equally embody your essential nature at work, in your intimate relationships, or with family and friends. In other words, you may not walk your talk. The more you embody what you know yourself to be, the more your every action becomes a radiant expression of truth.

• **Living the awakened life (Chapter 10).** Once your awakening has deepened and clarified and has come to inform every moment of your life, you naturally and spontaneously act in alignment with your deepest truth. Seeing the inherent emptiness of self and the essential inseparability of self and other, you no longer feel moved to act out of narrow self-interest but instead follow the flow of life itself, acting in attunement with the movement of the whole, the Tao.

HOW TO READ THIS BOOK

If these stages don't make much sense to you right now, don't worry—I've telescoped a lifetime of insight and realization into a few short pages, and we'll spend the rest of this book exploring, elaborating, and deepening the same fundamental principles. In fact, I'll be repeating the same truths again and again so they can gradually bypass your mind and awaken your own inner knowing, the deeper dimension inside you that already knows who you are.

For the purpose of supporting these teachings in their work of awakening, you might experiment with a new way of reading and listening to them—that is, not with your mind, but with your whole being. Just as you listen to a beautiful piece of music—whether it's a sonata by Mozart or a song by Madonna—by opening your ears and allowing the music to move and affect you at a visceral level, you can read this book with the same attitude. Don't try to figure it out, compare it with other books you've read, or filter it through a collection of preconceived ideas. Just relax your body, set aside your judgments, and let the words act on you. They carry the energy and music of their source—let them resonate inside you.

Awakening doesn't happen through effort or will, but by being what my teacher Jean Klein used to call *disponible*, a French word meaning "available, or receptive," to truth. The less you do, the better; no need to make sense of what I say on a conceptual level. Over time, the teachings will keep returning to you unbidden at unexpected moments in your everyday life, perhaps to bring light to a particular circumstance or challenge, or merely to illuminate another aspect of truth. The fact is, the awakening process, once begun, develops its own momentum without effort on your part, and the truth naturally yearns to awaken to itself through you. Eventually, after repeated listening, the truth will spontaneously spring to life inside you, and you'll recognize that it has always belonged to you, has always been the essential truth of your being; it's just been hidden from view.

As an invitation for you to be receptive and available to truth, I've included several guided meditations in each chapter. The "Breathe and Reflect" exercises, which appear intermittently, provide an opportunity to pause, let your analytical mind relax for a few moments, and reflect on the truth of what you're reading. The "Wake-Up Calls" at the end of each chapter are prolonged meditations intended to bypass the mind and allow you to glimpse the deeper truth behind the words. Use these exercises not as repetitive daily practices or more items on your interminable to-do list, but as sporadic forays into uncharted terrain, laboratory experiments with the potential to reveal some new and enlightening insights. Do them as you feel inclined. Just follow the instructions with beginner's mind, and notice how the exercise affects you.

Ultimately, nothing I say in this book is true in any lasting way—it's just an expedient means, a pointer, to turn your attention inward to the source of all teachings. Because truth is essentially nondual and includes everything without exception, anything I assert about it is both true and false— and neither true nor false. For example, if I say that the truth of your being is profound silence, I may awaken this silence inside you but ignore the fact that truth ultimately includes noise as well. If I call it "stillness," I neglect the dynamic flow of truth in manifestation, the rush and urgency of life in all its fullness. If I say "joy," I leave out the sorrow of the human condition. If I call it a "precious jewel," I ignore the heap of refuse by the side of the road that shines with the radiance of being. For this reason, the teachings throughout this book are filled with paradoxes—indeed, paradox is the only way to approach truth with the respect it deserves. Again, don't try to resolve these paradoxes or figure them out—let them bypass your mind and act on your whole being. As the American sage and poet Walt Whitman said, "Do I contradict myself? Very well then, I contradict myself. I am large, I contain multitudes."

1

ENTERING
THE GATELESS GATE

Truly, is anything missing right now?
Nirvana is right here, before your eyes.
This very place is the Lotus Land,
This very body is the body of the Buddha.

—*Zen Master Hakuin, "The Song of Zazen"*

*S*everal months before I turned sixteen, my mother died
suddenly in an automobile accident. As I struggled to come
to terms with this heart-wrenching loss, I found myself
losing something equally precious as well—my faith in the
benevolent, omniscient God who had guided and cared
for me since childhood. My whole world of belonging and
meaning collapsed within a few weeks. Grief-stricken and
bereft, I didn't have the support necessary to help me process my feelings. So I turned to the world of philosophy to
help me deal with my pain.

In the American transcendentalists, I discovered intimations of a more mysterious, impersonal divinity that infused,
animated, and yet transcended all things. From Ralph Waldo

Emerson and Henry David Thoreau, I made my way to German idealists like Immanuel Kant and Arthur Schopenhauer, who challenged my conventional way of knowing reality and pointed to a fundamental principle prior to thought. Learning that these philosophers had been influenced by the wisdom of Asia, I soon found myself on the doorstep of Buddhism and Zen.

In those days, books on Buddhism were scarce and often difficult to decipher. But in the few Zen books I could lay my hands on, I found images of masters who sat unperturbed as earthquakes rumbled around them and samurai swordsmen threatened to cut off their heads. Troubled by the pain of a difficult childhood and a longing for the mother-love I had recently lost, I desperately desired to transcend my suffering and awaken to the unshakable tranquillity and equanimity these men and women had apparently achieved. After several years of reading, including college courses in Asian philosophy and experimentation with mind-altering drugs, I finally looked up *Zen* in the phone book and began weekly trips to a little Zen center in midtown Manhattan for an evening of meditation and spiritual talk.

COMING HOME

On one particularly warm summer evening, as the pungent smell of Japanese incense filled the meditation hall, one of the roshi's senior students, a woman my mother's age, gave a talk that ignited a fire deep inside me and set me off on the pathless path. "Zazen [Zen meditation]," she said softly, "is the way to bring you to your long-lost home." As a college student with no home to return to and no sense of a stable center or home within, I was profoundly touched by these words. I yearned to discover my true home, the one I knew could never be lost.

In that moment more than thirty years ago, I came face-to-face for the first time with the core paradox at the heart of the spiritual journey. According to the books I read and the teachings I received, the home I so fervently sought existed right here and now, inside me. Being home, after all, it wasn't some exotic and unfamiliar Garden of Eden, but the place I inherently belonged, my birthright, my natural state, the awakened nature that already shone forth from inside me. I was being told that Zen meditation was the way to go there, even though there was apparently nowhere to go. My mind simply couldn't wrap itself around this paradox, so I took the easy way out and shifted my focus from discovering home to counting my breaths.

Many years later, when I finally did come home once and for all, I realized that I had never been apart from it even for an instant. As one of my teachers liked to say, it's your nearest, your home ground, the silent presence gazing through these eyes, giving rise to these thoughts, animating these arms and legs. Not the me you take yourself to be, but the one you really are—the mysterious, ungraspable subject of all objects, the "I am" prior to all characteristics. Yet somehow my true home, apparently as near as breath itself, had remained completely invisible to me, even though my teachers kept pointing toward it (as I'm doing now). As a result, I ended up searching for more than twenty years, sitting long

Breathe and Reflect

Close your eyes, and imagine yourself abiding in your true home, wherever that may be. Take a few moments to experience this home in all your senses—the sights, the sounds, the smells. How do you feel? Where do you feel it? Are you surprised in any way by the feelings and images that the word *home* evokes?

hours in meditation, listening to countless teachings, reading innumerable books, before I found myself where I had always been.

In our heart of hearts, don't we all yearn to return home, not to the family of our childhood, but to the place where we feel completely free to be ourselves—a place of total contentment, relaxation, and ease? You may never have experienced such a home on this earthly plane, yet you may have glimpsed the possibility from time to time. Perhaps you've had such intimations walking on the beach, listening to music, or lying entwined in the arms of a beloved—a fleeting few moments of indescribable peace and love, when time seemed to stop, space opened up, and you encountered something indescribably sacred and profound. But such experiences inevitably come and go, and you may have been left believing that you could never experience such peace consistently from moment to moment. Or you may have been so enthralled by the encounter that you spent years trying to re-create it through spiritual teachings and practices.

This paradox of the home we've never left but must somehow rediscover is expressed throughout the world's spiritual traditions by the universal parable of the prodigal son. Wandering off from his father's home in search of some distant treasure, the prodigal forgets who he is and inadvertently stumbles home years later, where he is found by his father, welcomed back, and offered his original inheritance and birthright. In one version of the story, he finds a treasure map that leads him back home to the jewel buried beneath his own hearth. In another, the prodigal, who has been reduced to poverty, discovers a precious diamond that was hidden in his pocket all along.

These versions of the parable acknowledge the mystery of the spiritual journey: there's no place to go but here, yet the going is often inevitable because it wears us out, humbles us, and prepares us to receive the treasure with a gratitude and appreciation we might not otherwise have experienced. By looking to externals for answers and coming up empty again and again, we discover everything we're not—pleasurable experiences, material possessions, spiritual accomplishments, blissful mind-states, anything that comes and goes—and become more open to recognizing what we really are, the indestructible jewel of true nature, which as Jesus said is beyond rust and decay.

ENCOUNTERING THE GATELESS GATE

This paradoxical dance of seeking and finding wears different costumes in different traditions. In Zen, it's usually known as the "gateless gate." Until you crack the combination and pass through, you can't fully understand the meaning of the great Zen teachings, but all your mental effort inevitably proves fruitless before this enigmatic and impenetrable barrier. You need to bring your whole being to the process, not just your mind, and allow the paradox to transform you from inside. Many Zen koans pose some version of this paradox, disorienting the mind and evoking an answer from another dimension of knowing.

Consider the famous saying attributed to Shakyamuni Buddha: "All beings are inherently enlightened, but because of their attachments and distorted views, they can't realize this fact." I can still remember how these words short-circuited my mind the first time I heard them. "If we can't realize it, then how can we possibly say we're enlightened?" I mused. "But if we're really enlightened, why can't we realize it?"

As a neophyte practitioner, I understood these words to mean that deep down inside me there was this enlightened nature that I somehow needed to discover, and meditation was a kind of excavation project designed to unearth it. For years I kept digging, sitting intensive retreats, contemplating koans, emptying my mind to make room for the influx of awakening. I was spurred on in this archeological exploration by my teachers, who offered encouragement in private interviews and lavished authority and cachet on those who passed koans quickly. Eventually I just wore myself out with the digging, so I set aside my shovel (and my monk's robes) and went back to living a more ordinary life. Yet the paradox continued to gnaw at me silently, from the inside.

The fact is, once you're gripped by the core paradox and recognize that consensus, everyday reality is merely a reflection of some deeper truth that's close at hand but hidden from view, you've embarked on a search that you can never really abandon, no matter how far you seem to stray. The Zen masters say that encountering the paradox is like swallowing a red-hot iron ball you can neither disgorge nor pass through. Until you digest it, you can never be completely at peace.

Throughout the centuries, zealous Zen students have meditated long hours struggling to resolve this paradox, to return home, to discover their "original face." In the Rinzai Zen tradition, practitioners bellow, "*Mu*" (the key word from one of the most important koans) for hours in their fervor to break through the gate. The tradition's stories are filled with notable examples of those who took their practice to even greater extremes, standing in the snow for hours, sitting at the edge of a precipice, walking on foot from master to master. "Monasteries are places for desperate people," my first Zen teacher used to say, by which he meant people whose suffering, urgency, or intensity drives them forward on their long and often lonely search.

Many centuries ago, the Persian mystic poet Rumi described his own divine desperation in these words:

I have lived on the lip
of insanity, wanting to know reasons,
knocking on a door. It opens.
I've been knocking from the inside!

Judging from this poem, Rumi struggles for a long time to penetrate the paradox with his mind, but the door eventually opens by itself, almost in spite of his efforts, and reveals that he's been living in the secret chamber all along. Rumi's epiphany when he discovers that he's been looking from the inside out mirrors the surprise, relief, and delight of those seekers who wear themselves out attempting to unravel the paradox and drop to the ground exhausted, only to discover that they've never strayed from home, even in their most desperate moments. "No creature ever falls short of its own completeness," says Zen master Dogen. "Wherever it stands, it does not fail to cover the ground."

Needless to say, this intense longing to crack the code and reveal the truth at the heart of reality is as ancient and universal as humankind itself. You could say that it's in our DNA. According to the Sufis, God said to the Prophet Muhammad, "I am a hidden treasure, and I want to be known." In his yearning to be loved and experienced, God set in motion an evolutionary pattern that reached its pinnacle in the human capacity for spiritual awakening. God, or Truth, in other words, is seeking to awaken to itself through you, to see itself everywhere through your eyes and taste itself everywhere through your lips. "That which you are seeking," wrote an anonymous sage, "is always seeking you."

Ultimately, your every desire—the desire for material things, relationships, career success, sexual gratification—is really the desire for the peace you experience for brief moments when you attain the object of your desire. Of course, such conditional peace is fleeting, and you move restlessly on to new objects and new desires in the hope of recapturing it. Until you know who you really are, know the freedom from desire that's the true aim of every desire, you can never recognize the peace that can never be disturbed or lost.

ESCAPING FROM THE PRISON

Though many people seem to "effort" and struggle for years to rediscover their innate awakened nature, others just seem to stumble on it inadvertently, without intensive meditation or deep inquiry. One friend of mine realized the emptiness of self quite unexpectedly while boarding a bus. Another asked the question "Who am I?" just once and penetrated through the illusion of a separate self. Still another woke up one morning without her accustomed identity; instead, pure awareness seemed to move through her body and experience life through her senses. But if you're like Rumi, you need to exhaust yourself with the knocking.

There's a traditional story about a man imprisoned for a crime he didn't commit who attempts to dig his way to freedom with a spoon—rather like the character played by Tim Robbins in *The Shawshank Redemption*. After years of bone-wearying struggle, his hands calloused and bloody, he finally realizes the futility of his efforts and gives up. Tears of frustration and desperation streaming down his cheeks, he leans back against the door of his cell, only to discover that it's been unlocked all along. No doubt his surprise and relief are similar to Rumi's. As implausible as this story may seem, the point is clear—the prison that you imagine constrains you doesn't really exist.

Indeed, the one who tries by every available means to escape from the prison is the prison itself, as my teacher Jean Klein used to say. This formulation points directly to the source of our imprisonment—the mind that believes we're imprisoned! Whether you can look directly at the source of the prison and release yourself from its grasp in the looking, or need to wear yourself out pounding on the bars, depends more on your karma than on your intentions. Even those who attempt to go directly to the source may suddenly find themselves confused and disoriented, standing once again outside the gate. "The only obstacle to complete realization is the thought 'I have not realized,'" said the great Indian sage Ramana Maharshi, but dispensing with that pesky thought can be the work of a lifetime.

THE OPEN SECRET

Some spiritual traditions, including Advaita Vedanta, refer to the core paradox as the "open secret": The truth of your being has never been hidden from view—indeed, it's as plain as the nose on your face—yet it remains a secret because you don't know how and where to look, and the teacher's job is to point you in the right direction. Instead of being advised to storm the barrier or crack the code through intensive practices, you're counseled to listen to the teachings and allow them to point you gently in the right direction. Then, in a moment out of time, the secret reveals itself to you.

In fact, the nose on your face is actually invisible when you're looking straight ahead; you have to maneuver your eyes in a particular way if you want to see it. You're accustomed to focusing on external objects but rarely turn around to look at the one who looks, the source of all seeing. "The eye can't see the eye," the sages say, because it's the medium through which you see. Yet you can come to know the eye in a subtler and more indirect way, can apperceive the source of seeing, through a direct and timeless recognition that bypasses the mind.

The process is rather like solving a figure-ground puzzle where it's difficult to distinguish the image from the background. You pore over the picture with curiosity and perhaps a little perplexity, until you suddenly realize that the vase you've been staring at is also two faces touching; once you see the faces, you wonder how you could ever have missed them. Or like rummaging around the house before an important appointment, frantically searching for your keys, only to discover that they were buried in your pocket all along. Or even more embarrassing, like hunting for your sunglasses until someone points out that they're already perched on top of your head. "Ah, here they are," you say. "I knew they were there somewhere." The recognition is immediate and quite ordinary—like opening the door to your home and stepping through.

ABSOLUTE AND RELATIVE TRUTHS

Beneath the paradoxical metaphors of the open secret and the gateless gate lies a crucial philosophical distinction common to both Buddhism and Advaita Vedanta: the two truths. At the level of absolute, or ultimate, truth, you're already enlightened, already Buddha, already perfect and complete just the way you are, and everything in every direction shines with the same inherent perfection. Nothing needs to be added or taken away, figured out or improved, because nothing is ever problematic. Past and future, cause and effect, do not exist, only this timeless moment, the eternal Now, in which manifest reality is constantly springing forth in some mysterious and ungraspable way. At the level of relative, or conventional, truth, you may not enjoy the peace and contentment of Buddhahood because you haven't yet recognized your inherent perfection, and you read teachings and engage in practices in order to experience the ultimate for yourself. Problems are constantly arising and requiring your attention, situations demand improvement, and reality (at least at the superatomic level) closely follows the law of cause and effect.

Both truths apply simultaneously; rather than being mutually exclusive, they're inseparable, and the goal of the spiritual enterprise is to acknowledge and embrace them both. In fact, they're merely flip sides of the same nondual reality that includes both the personal realm of thoughts and feelings and the transpersonal realm of pure awareness; the apparent world of work, family, and relationships and the essential world where everything is merely an expression of the One. Even using words like *realms, worlds,* and *levels* gives the mistaken impression that they're separate in some way, which they're not. The Heart Sutra says that form is emptiness, and emptiness is form, in a formulation we'll be exploring again and again. Form is no other than emptiness, and emptiness no other than form. The mind can't wrap itself around this paradoxical truth—you can only experience it directly, beyond the mind.

As an example, take your closest relationship. If you see yourself and your partner or friend only as two separate personalities attempting to learn your life lessons and maximize your potential for growth and

> ### *Breathe and Reflect*
>
> Take a few moments to consider this paradox, but don't try to figure it out with the mind. Instead, let your body resonate to the phrase "form is emptiness, emptiness is form." Notice how your body responds.

development, you will definitely achieve a certain level of intimacy. But you may miss the deeper experience of knowing that the two of you are already essentially one and that love is who you both are fundamentally, beneath the personal issues. When you embrace both truths, you can have the freedom and equanimity that comes with seeing the empty, luminous, dreamlike nature of these two apparently separate selves and at the same time enjoy the tenderness and openness that comes with recognizing the humanness and vulnerability that this sacred emptiness has chosen to express through these forms. Only in the presence of both the absolute and relative truths, the spiritual and mundane dimensions, can the deepest intimacy flourish.

STRAYING AWAY FROM HOME— AND RETURNING

If you've never left home even for an instant, why do you appear to stray, forget who you really are, and struggle to find your way back again? Believe it or not, this age-old question does not seem to have a satisfactory answer. "Holding a begging bowl, a man with amnesia knocks on his own door," says the Indian poet Kabir.

As children, we spend much of our time in a kind of perpetual openness and wonder, attuned to the magic and mystery that plays beneath the surface of life. Many people have intimations of their true nature in childhood—the sense of a benevolent presence guiding their life, a radiance that shines forth from all things, or a current of love that unites us all. In his "Ode: Intimations of Immortality," William Wordsworth puts it well:

> There was a time when meadow, grove, and stream,
> The earth, and every common sight,
> To me did seem
> Apparell'd in celestial light,
> The glory and the freshness of a dream.

But as he goes on to bemoan, we lose touch with this luminosity as we age and eventually realize that we can no longer recapture it.

Whatever causes this wandering and ultimate return, it seems to be inevitable, like the journey of the prodigal son. Growing up in a consensus reality that emphasizes the individual, taught to believe we're inadequate and need to "make something" of ourselves (whatever that could possibly mean), chastised for some behaviors (our shortcomings) and praised for others (our virtues), we lose touch with the expansiveness of being and end up believing that we're this separate skin-bound little me, this fraction of the whole, that the world has encouraged us to be.

Over time, we accumulate more and more beliefs, stories, and memories that shroud the radiance of being we experienced as children. The simple joy and boundless potential that comes with realizing "I am" gets burdened with a lifetime of acquired identities and characteristics, the limited parts we play in the drama of life: "I'm a parent, a sinner, a healer, a slow learner, a good friend, a failure, depressed, extroverted, attractive," and so on. In other words, we forget who we really are and succumb to the way others see us until one day, perhaps, we have intimations of our immortality, our timeless spiritual nature, become seekers, and embark on the return journey home. "From my home in the hills, why did I roam?" laments singer/songwriter Jai Uttal. "To my home in the hills take me back."

Why do we have to lose touch with our spiritual home? Why can't we just remember who we are, rather than going through the painful process of straying and returning?

Who knows? "Why" questions are the mind's attempt to make sense of the incomprehensible. The only truly honest answer is, because that's the way it is. Some traditions say that God is playing games with himself. What we do know is that just about everyone strays from his or her "home in the hills," though there are rare individuals who never lose touch with their divine nature through childhood and adulthood. Wordsworth says, "Our birth is a sleep and a forgetting," and many sages agree that the mere act of being born in human form causes us to lose touch with who we are.

But couldn't we bring up children in such a way that we could avoid this process?

We can do our best to avoid imposing our ideas and beliefs on our children and give them plenty of room to be who they are, and of course, we can support them in their innocence, openness, and wonder. But eventually they will succumb to the intense cultural pressure to identify as a separate self. It seems to be inevitable, and so therefore is the process of straying and returning.

If you want to influence the next generation, the most important thing you can do is to awaken yourself. Embody the possibility of freedom in your own life, and you will have a profound effect on the people around you.

Is it necessary to wrestle with what you call the "core paradox" in order to awaken? Somehow the paradox doesn't really resonate for me.

Not at all. Awakening doesn't require any particular practice or contemplation, though some seekers have found that grappling with this paradox has apparently precipitated an awakening. Even a sincere curiosity or earnest interest in discovering the truth of existence—which has been recommended by many teachers, including my own—is not a prerequisite. As I describe later in this book, some people awaken without the slightest interest or preparation, and others don't, despite years of practice. Paradoxical, isn't it?

What about suffering? You mention the importance of suffering in your own search. Can I awaken without intense suffering?

Again, suffering is not required, but it does have the uncanny ability to pull the rug out from beneath your comfortable little world and open you to a deeper source of meaning and fulfillment. It's a powerful motivator. You don't have to go looking for it, of course—it will find you eventually.

Wake-Up Call

Is There Anything Missing Right Now?

Set aside ten to fifteen minutes for this exploration. Begin by sitting comfortably for a few moments with your eyes open. As you gaze around the room, notice how your mind judges and interprets what you see. "The furniture looks shabby. The papers are out of place. The carpet's stained. The bills need to be paid." Your mind is constantly making comments like these, adding a conceptual overlay that makes it difficult for you to experience reality directly. Even concepts like "book" and "table" limit your ability to see beyond the form to the underlying essence of what is.

Now close your eyes and slowly open them again. This time gaze around you as if you were an extraterrestrial who's just landed on Earth or an infant who's just been born. Look at the window, the computer, the carpet, as if you've never seen them before and have no idea what they are. Enjoy the play of light and dark, color and form, movement and stillness, without giving names to the display. Allow yourself to abide in a natural state of wonder and awe. You have no idea what anything is. Notice how this innocent, open looking acts on your being.

After about ten minutes of innocent looking, gently ask yourself, "On present evidence, without consulting the mind, is there anything missing or lacking in my experience right now?" If this question makes no sense to you, just let it go and continue your looking. If your mind starts recounting a familiar story about what you apparently need but don't have, about how your life is lacking or inadequate in some way, set it aside and go back to simply looking. Remember, you've been asked to consult present evidence only.

Now ask the question again—"On present evidence, without consulting the mind, is there anything missing or lacking in my experience right now?"—and allow an answer to emerge. If you finally conclude that nothing is missing or lacking, notice how this realization changes your experience of what is. If this isn't your conclusion, just continue asking, allowing an answer to emerge and returning to innocent looking.

2

SEEKING WITHOUT A SEEKER

> There is no greater mystery than this, that we keep
> seeking reality though in fact we are reality.
>
> —*Ramana Maharshi*

The truth of your being is ordinary, simple, and ever-present. As *A Course in Miracles* says, "It takes no time to be who you are." Each moment offers you an opportunity to recognize the silent, awake presence that's always already right here and now, underlying your experience and illuminating all things. Yet no matter how clearly and repeatedly I describe this truth to you, no matter how many terms and metaphors I use, you're not likely to feel satisfied until you experience this truth directly for yourself. As the old adage goes, images of cakes just can't satisfy hunger—you have to taste the real thing, enjoy its sweetness and texture, feel the crumbs in your mouth. This paradox is the open secret, the gateless gate: Buddha nature, Christ consciousness, Big Mind, pure spirit is who you essentially are, but you won't experience the happiness and fulfillment you seek until you meet it face-to-face.

Of course, you can't find what you already are the way you find a new relationship or a better job—by networking with other people, making phone calls, surfing the Web. Even reading spiritual books can take you only so far, to the starting line where the real search begins. In fact, when you know from the outset that what you're seeking is right here and now, as available and intimate as breath—indeed, that it's your birthright, your natural state, which can't be fabricated or achieved—your search tends to take on a different focus. You may find it more difficult to seek outside yourself in deities or gurus for the source of your fulfillment or to attempt to attain it by cultivating mind-states or manufacturing experiences. In the light of the teaching that you already are what you seek, any effort to go somewhere else or be something you're not seems misguided and heavy-handed. Instead, the search tends to become subtler and more paradoxical, less like an arduous heroic quest and more like a silent attunement, an inner listening.

But such inner attunement can be difficult to maintain without the support of a teacher. As a result, many seekers, even those who are acquainted with the open secret, are enticed to seek outside themselves in clear-cut practices and paths for a more forceful way through. Somehow, this outward search and ultimate return appear to be unavoidable, just as the prodigal son of the parable had to leave home in order to rediscover the treasure under his own hearth. "The truth cannot be found through seeking, but only seekers find it," goes the old saying. In other words, you just may need to don the mantle of the seeker and set out on the path, even though you've been told that what you seek is already right here. In the end, however, you have to exhaust all of your strategies and give up the search for the truth to reveal itself to you.

Often the search begins with a genuine intimation of truth, a momentary peek behind the veil of illusion that piques your curiosity and whets your appetite for more. Maybe you encounter teachings that resonate inside you and elicit a "felt" sense of some deeper reality. Or maybe you have a full-blown spiritual experience—your mind suddenly stops for no apparent reason and you sense the silent observer that's always been watching the thoughts come and go. Or your body dissolves and you recognize the empty nature of all phenomena. But the experience inevitably dissipates, and you're left with a longing to re-create or rediscover it, perhaps even to push beyond it to your essential nature, the true source of every spiritual experience.

At this point, you're about to set foot on the pathless path home, and you may naturally begin to orient yourself like an animal in the forest, sniffing for the trail and looking around for guidance and support on your journey. If you're fortunate enough to meet a teacher of the direct approach to truth who tells you to stop, relax, listen to what's already present, and turn your attention toward the experiencer behind the experience, you may be able to awaken directly without prolonged seeking. But if you're like most people, you'll be drawn by the promise of spiritual adventure to thumb through the pages of spiritual magazines; Google spiritual key words; or wander through the spirituality section of your local bookstore or Amazon.com in search of the right book, teacher, or community. The options are appealing and mind-boggling in their number and diversity. Everywhere you turn you're offered spiritual fulfillment if you're willing to sign on to a set of practices and invest your trust in a particular approach.

Cultivate mindfulness and loving-kindness with an Asian-trained teacher of Vipassana (insight) meditation, and eventually you may develop the qualities of heart and mind necessary to attain the "other shore" of enlightenment. Chant and pray with a Hindu guru in the Indian tradition of bhakti yoga, and God may grant you the grace of a kundalini awakening. Engage in preliminary practices and deity visualizations under the guidance of a Buddhist teacher born and trained in old Tibet, and you may be fortunate enough to be reborn as a buddha in some future lifetime.

From a direct intuition of the imminent availability of the truth of your being, you've been lured into the spiritual marketplace, where well-intentioned vendors hawk their wares, promising enlightenment somewhere in the distant future as the result of years of effort if you're willing to buy their product, take their course, join their community, and invest thousands of hours of your time. The innocent initial impulse to orient, listen, and move toward truth the way a child naturally returns to its mother or a bird to its nesting ground has been co-opted by an established tradition and turned into a circuitous path to spiritual realization. Welcome to the progressive approach!

THE PROS AND CONS OF PROGRESSION

Progressive paths are extraordinarily appealing because they've been so carefully elaborated, often over many centuries. Bearing the imprimatur of an established tradition, they suggest that if you just follow the instructions wholeheartedly, the results will take care of themselves. If you listen to enough teachings, spend enough hours in meditation, attend enough retreats, cultivate enough of the right attitudes and qualities, you'll one day discover the truth of who you really are. As inspiration, the progressive scriptures are filled with exhortatory tales of masters who began as seekers just like you and me and eventually achieved enlightenment through prolonged and concerted effort.

The progressive approach can be quite comforting to the mind, which doesn't like uncertainty and wants to know where you're headed and how to get there. At the same time, it appeals to the ego's love of a good struggle. Indeed, the ego—the separate self-sense you mistakenly take yourself to be—views itself as the embattled hero of the drama called life and the spiritual path as the ultimate hero's journey, with Buddha under the bodhi tree replacing Ulysses or Rocky Balboa. After years of effort, the ego imagines, you too can sit on the pinnacle of realization, in the asana of complete repose, flashing the mudras of fearlessness and peace.

Progression provides you with something noble and meaningful to do, a beneficial lifestyle, a community of fellow seekers, a sense of belonging. You can learn to enjoy a vegetarian diet, participate in the life of an ashram or a meditation center, reap the health benefits of regular meditation or yoga practice, read Dharma books, listen to spiritual music, feel yourself to be a part of a growing global movement of spiritual awareness. No wonder so many seekers are drawn to enlist.

As benign as it may seem, however, the gradual approach to spiritual unfolding may actually undermine the possibility of awakening right now, for a number of significant reasons. When you're encouraged to shift your focus from awakening to the practice that will purportedly lead you to awakening, you may end up devoting years to perfecting the form and becoming an accomplished meditator or yoga practitioner without ever awakening to the truth that's so close at hand. Some Buddhists I know, for example, have spent decades wearing robes, following their breaths, and giving Dharma talks without ever having a convincing glimpse of their essential nature, their original face. The danger of investing your energy in seeking is that you'll end up a perpetual seeker, without ever finding what you were looking for in the first place.

Perhaps even more fundamentally, the very premise of the progressive approach—that you need to engage in certain practices over a period of time in order to realize who you are—reinforces the belief that your true nature is deeply concealed and requires protracted effort to uncover. I spent many years on my meditation cushion, sitting with upright posture and clasped hands, struggling to catch a fleeting glimpse of my true nature, as if it were some rare animal or bird hidden behind the tangled undergrowth of thoughts.

Eventually, after giving up the effort and the formal practice of meditation, I met a teacher who told me, "The seeker is the sought; the looker is what he or she is looking for." My mind couldn't wrap itself around these words, but one day soon after, in a moment out of time, the seeker and the sought collapsed into one another, and I knew who I was once and for all. The one who had been looking so hard for true nature was the very true nature I had been looking for. Truth had been playing hide-and-seek with itself. As long as I continued focusing so much effort on searching, I couldn't possibly stumble backward into the silent presence that was the source of all searching.

Did my years of meditation make me more susceptible to awakening? It's impossible to tell. I do know that the awakening happened after I'd stopped meditating regularly. Proponents of the progressive approach generally claim that their particular technique—whether it's mindfulness meditation, mantra recitation, or hatha yoga—has been refined over centuries by countless masters and teachers as a vehicle to bring you closer to truth. As evidence, they point to the many enlightened members of their lineage. But what about the thousands of nameless and faceless practitioners who spent years in the monastery and never had so much as a glimpse of enlightenment? Or by contrast, the many great spiritual adepts who woke up without any techniques or methods? Ramana Maharshi, the world-renowned twentieth-century Indian sage, pretended he was dying at the age of sixteen and within a half an hour had dropped his identity as a separate self and awakened as the Self of all. (Interest-

ingly enough, he never prescribed this practice to others.)
Hui-neng, the Sixth Patriarch of Chinese Zen, became
enlightened shortly before entering the monastery, upon
hearing a verse from the Diamond Sutra. Even the Buddha's
enlightenment did not result from arduous practice, despite
what tradition suggests. On the contrary, it apparently
occurred only after he gave up his ascetic practice, accepted
some nourishing food, and sat down on a comfortable bed
of grass in the shade of a tree, vowing not to get up until he
reached the end of his search. Clearly, progressive practices
are not necessary for awakening to occur.

In fact, the prolonged practice of a particular technique
may have the opposite effect, deadening and habituating
the mind, rather than making it more open and accessible to truth. If you want to know how a progressive path
might affect you, spend some time at one of the tradition's
residential meditation centers or ashrams. Do the longtime
practitioners appear happier, freer, more peaceful, more
enlightened? Or do they seem rigid in their adherence to
structures and rules, lacking in spontaneity, proud of their
spiritual progress or stature, addicted to control? Every
center, tradition, and practitioner is different, of course, but
many of the ashrams and monasteries I've visited lack the joy
and aliveness one would expect to find there; instead, they
exude a quality of emotional repression and subservience
to form.

Now I'm not suggesting that spiritual practice isn't enor-
mously beneficial at many levels. Studies have shown that
the regular practice of meditation, for example, can reduce

your heart rate, lower your blood pressure and cholesterol levels, boost your immune system, increase your longevity, and enhance your overall enjoyment of life. The problem lies not with the technique, but with the attitude or orientation with which it's practiced. If you view your practice as a gradual means to some distant and lofty goal, you may lose your initial passion, enthusiasm, and curiosity and miss the open secret of your true nature in your dogged determination to accumulate spiritual experiences and become a more spiritual person. My teacher Jean Klein used to say, "Don't make meditation a habit," lest your practice become lifeless and dull. Instead, enter your meditation as you would a laboratory, with the express intention of finding the meditator.

Recently, I reconnected with an old Buddhist friend who exemplifies some of the pitfalls of the progressive approach. Originally drawn to spiritual practice by her intense desire to transcend her suffering, Michele spent years studying with a particular teacher while raising two children and working as a chiropractor. As she developed into a seasoned meditator, she also became entrenched in a particular identity as a senior student in the hierarchy of the tradition, one who had logged a certain number of years on her cushion and supposedly reached a certain level of spiritual maturity. Although now in the position of guiding others, she has never had more than a fleeting glimpse of true nature herself, and she no longer has access to her teacher, who died more than ten years ago. In a sense, you could say that she's reached a dead end on the progressive path. After so many years, she has become a better person—calmer,

more self-aware, less emotionally reactive or stressed out,
more content—but she hasn't experienced the realization
she originally sought. In fact, she's given up believing that
the practice she spent so many years cultivating can actually bring her the profound peace and joy that the Buddhist
stories promise. But she's a teacher herself now, a senior
student, and doesn't feel comfortable leaving the fold and
exploring other approaches or meeting other teachers. So
she soldiers on with a certain measure of disappointment
and resignation, secretly convinced that deep and abiding
awakening isn't possible for her.

Michele's initial urgent impulse to awaken was chan-
neled by the tradition into years of devotion to a path that
in the end did not fulfill its original promise. In the process,
she imbibed a system of beliefs about what awakening looks
like and how it's achieved that just made it seem like a distant, unachievable goal—and made it more difficult for her
to open to the possibility that her true nature is ever-present
and readily accessible right now. If only she could complete
these practices, solve these riddles, master these texts, she
was taught, then she could discover who she really is.

Over the years, Michele focused her energies on becoming a better person by gradually calming her mind and cultivating more spiritual qualities like patience, equanimity,
loving-kindness, and generosity, with the understanding
that such qualities would bring her closer to enlightenment.
But no amount of effort can bring you closer to who you
are—after all, it's your nearest, as intimate as breath—and
the belief that you need to effort just takes you further away

because it causes you to stray from what's already so close at hand. "Don't you see," asked the Indian teacher Nisargadatta Maharaj, "that your very search for happiness is what makes you feel miserable?" The cultivation of so-called spiritual qualities just plays into the mind's most cherished assumption—one that receives widespread reinforcement in our self-improvement culture—that there's something wrong with you as you are, and you need to become a better you before you can be the real you. Deep down, you believe that you're inherently flawed, especially when you compare yourself to the great exemplars of your tradition, and you keep efforting to live up to some image of how you think you're supposed to think, feel, and act. In Zen, this attitude is called putting another head on top of your own, rather than enjoying the perfectly good head you already have.

Perhaps most insidious, years of dedication to gradual cultivation just strengthen the grip of the seeker—the separate someone who negotiates the path, attends the retreats, accumulates the insights, has the experiences, racks up the spiritual points. Ironic as it may seem, spiritual people who are apparently devoted to releasing the hold of the ego and experiencing the emptiness of self can, in the process, develop enormous spiritual egos that lie hidden and unexamined in the shadows. "Look at how calm, centered, loving, and peaceful I've become," the little voice whispers as it charts your progress. Or on a more negative note, "I just can't seem to get the knack of meditation. Even though I've been practicing for years, I don't seem to be making any progress." Once this seeker identity has become deeply entrenched, it

Breathe and Reflect

Take a few moments to reflect on your own approach to seeking. If you've followed a progressive path, consider how it has affected your attitude toward spiritual awakening. Do you find that the practices have brought you closer to truth? What kinds of beliefs and stories do you tell yourself about the path you've chosen? If you're not currently pursuing a particular path, consider what draws you to spiritual seeking.

can be extremely difficult to see clearly and release, because the practices of the progressive approach tend to reinforce it by encouraging you to become a better, more spiritual you. Even the ultimate fruition of the progressive approach is inevitably dualistic, because it's claimed as an experience that belongs to the me—and the seeker never really dissolves, it merely becomes a finder.

THE DIRECT APPROACH—AND ITS SHADOW

Rather than proposing a gradual path of self-improvement as a means to self-realization, the direct approach I offer in this book points you immediately to your true nature right here and now—to the pure, eternal, unobstructed, boundless awareness that you always already are. You've never been apart from it even for an instant, so you can't possibly approach it, least of all by effort or progression. Just turn your attention back on itself and recognize your true faceless face once and for all.

The direct approach relies less on techniques than on the intimate relationship between teacher and student and the instantaneous transmission of truth from heart to heart and mind to mind—or as my first Zen teacher used to say, "from one warm hand to another." (The term *transmission* can give the mistaken impression that some knowledge or wisdom is passed from person to person. Rather, both teacher and student simultaneously share in and acknowledge the recognition of true nature.) Bodhidharma, the First Patriarch of Chinese Zen, called it a "special transmission outside the scriptures, no dependence on words and letters, pointing directly to the human heart, see true nature, become Buddha." In the Tibetan tradition known as Dzogchen ("great perfection"), teachers use "pointing-out instructions" to introduce their students to the essential nature of mind. In the Indian Advaita Vedanta tradition, sages use both words and silence to awaken their disciples to the living reality that's beyond both speech and silence. (The collective term for the Vedanta scriptures, *Upanishad*, literally means "to sit down near" the guru.) When my teacher told me, "The seeker is the sought," I didn't deliberately reflect on his words; they just took hold and transformed me from the inside, without conscious effort on my part.

Alas, the ego has the power to turn even the loveliest path into its own private toll road, and the direct approach also has its shadow side. Some folks, for example, think they can listen to a few teachings, read a few books, burn a little incense, dress in special clothing, and expect awakening to come knocking on their door without any sincere interest or inquiry. (It does happen, of course, but I wouldn't let your chai get cold waiting.) Others simply comprehend the teachings intellectually and then assume they've reached the end of their search. After all, the great sages say, "You are the Self always." In fact, these seekers are still standing outside the gateless gate, because halfhearted seeking, passive waiting, or mere conceptual understanding won't get them through. Still other aficionados of the direct approach become "professional seekers" who seem more interested in the personal comfort, meaning, and belonging they derive from their new identity than in the potential discomfort of genuine, transformative awakening, which tends to deconstruct even the most spiritual identities and reveal the living truth beneath.

SEEKING WITHOUT SEEKING

Yes, it's true that you can awaken to your true self in a moment out of time just by reading these words or listening to the teachings of the great sages of old. But generally it helps to be oriented, curious, dedicated, and even passionate about discovering who you really are. In other words, it helps to want truth more than anything else—and to know how and where to look.

The Sufis relate a parable in which the holy fool Nasruddin insists on looking for his keys under a lamppost because he has more light there, even though he lost them somewhere else. Although it's become something of a cliché, this story sheds some important light on the nature of the search. Like Nasruddin, you may be tempted to look for your true self outside yourself in the known, the tried and true, the familiar, because so many others have undertaken the journey before you and left so many lampposts there to light you on your way. Ultimately, however, your path is unique to you, and it begins in the darkness of not knowing and the simple yearning of your own heart. As Nisargadatta Maharaj said, "You must find your own way. Unless you find it yourself, it will not be your own way and will take you nowhere." You need to be willing to sit in this darkness, recognizing that the truth is hidden there, without immediately leaping to claim easy answers or proven practices. "To live in the known is bondage," adds Nisargadatta. "To live in the unknown is liberation."

The Upanishads describe three major doorways to truth: hearing, meditating, and pondering. The first (discussed in this chapter and the next) involves reading the sacred texts and listening to the words of a true teacher—not with the intention of gathering new concepts, but with a desire to experience the truth for yourself. The second (described in Chapter 4) involves welcoming whatever arises in your experience. And the third (discussed in Chapter 5) involves letting those words germinate inside you, in the fertile darkness of your own heart, while earnestly inquiring into the truth they express. Rather than effort or struggle, these three approaches require a quality of openness and receptivity, a willingness to put aside your preconceptions and experience reality directly, combined with a sincere dedication to discovering what's true once and for all. In other words, no matter how long your search lasts, it's crucial not to lose the freshness, vitality, and spontaneity of beginner's mind by turning your search into a lifeless habit, another item on the ego's endless self-improvement schedule. Remember that the separate self can never discover the truth—in the end, the truth just awakens to itself through you.

ARE YOU SURE YOU WANT TO DIE BEFORE YOU DIE?

The Tibetan teacher Chogyam Trungpa often warned his students to think twice before embarking on the spiritual path, because once they'd committed themselves, there would be no turning back—and nothing left of them when they were done. In the same spirit, I encourage you to ask yourself whether you're willing to give up everything you hold dear—your beliefs, your security, your familiar identity, your entire world of meaning—in order to awaken to your identity with the vastness of being. Once the wave realizes it's actually the ocean playing with itself, it can't go back to pretending it's just a wave anymore.

Everyone talks about spiritual awakening these days as if it were a pleasant experience you can simply add to your résumé, along with meditation retreats and yoga treks to India. But awakening, once it occurs, tends to be ruthless and uncontrollable, like a wildfire that burns up everything in its path. "Spirituality isn't child's play," warns Nisargadatta Maharaj. "My sentences will tear to pieces anyone who listens to them." After all, what you awaken to is the truth, which shatters the illusion of who you've believed yourself to be. You might want to consider whether you're ready to have your tidy little world torn to pieces or consumed in a conflagration before you set out to discover who you are. I've known many people whose lives were turned upside down by awakening and who spent years learning how to live in a completely new way. (In fact, this journey of waking up and then learning how to live your awakening is the subject of this book.) In Zen, enlightenment is affectionately known as the "Great Death," and practitioners are urged to "die before you die."

The Chinese tell a story about a man who loved dragons. He drew pictures of dragons, collected dragon statues, read everything he could possibly find about dragons. He was known far and wide as an expert on dragons. Then one day a

Breathe and Reflect

Spend some time considering whether you're ready to give up your familiar sense of self and your accustomed worldview for the sake of awakening to your true identity with something limitless and unknowable. Be ruthlessly honest with yourself. Of course, you don't need to make a commitment yet, and you don't have a choice in any case. You're either going to awaken or you're not. Just reflect on the profound, life-transforming consequences of spiritual awakening.

real dragon wandered by, stuck its head in his window, and breathed a little fire—and the terrified man ran off down the road and was never heard from again. Consider carefully before you cultivate an interest in awakening. Like the dragon, the experience can be fearsome, awe-inspiring, and life-changing, and it may take you in directions you never expected.

**Is some form of seeking or passionate inquiry really
necessary? What if I have no inclination to seek?**

If you're content with your life and don't feel a need to look
for something more, then by all means continue as you are.
I have no prescriptions to offer you, no self-improvement
schemes, no vested interest in trying to get you to awaken.
Seeking is optional, and so is finding. Just enjoy life as it is,
and be who you are.

**You mention the importance of a teacher's support.
But how do I choose a teacher? How can I tell
whether a teacher is authentic?**

As my teacher Jean Klein used to say, "You'll know you've met
a true teacher because you feel yourself in your autonomy
in his or her presence." That is, you feel freer to be yourself,
rather than feeling bound by the roles of teacher and student. The true teacher doesn't take the identity of teacher
seriously and doesn't need students to feel complete.

   In my first private interview with Jean, I was astonished
to discover that this person didn't take himself to be a
teacher—indeed, didn't take himself to be anyone at all—
and had absolutely no interest in making me his student, as
other teachers had. I was exhilarated because I no longer
felt required to live up to someone else's expectations. In the

presence of a true teacher, you feel freer, rather than more bound by rules and agendas.

How can I know whether I'm making progress or just wasting time on my spiritual path?

Where exactly are you trying to go? The whole notion of a path binds you to the belief that you're moving toward some distant goal. Call off the search and just be. Your mind may feel disoriented and frustrated at first because it doesn't know what to do, doesn't have any practices or techniques to apply, doesn't know how to measure its progress. But in the radiant spaciousness of your true nature, there's no place to go and nothing to achieve. You're already where you're supposed to be. Just enjoy this timeless moment, without expectation or manipulation, and awakening will take care of itself.

Wake-Up Call

What Are You Really Seeking?

Set aside ten to fifteen minutes for this exploration. Begin by sitting comfortably for a few minutes with your eyes closed. Now ask yourself the following questions: "What am I looking for? What's the goal of my search? How would I know if I found it? How would my life be different? What do I imagine enlightened people have that I don't?" Take some time to reflect on these questions. Be honest with yourself, and don't hold anything back. Perhaps you're looking for a quality of silent presence or nonjudgmental openness. Perhaps it's a peace and joy that's prior to the mind and can't be disturbed by thoughts or emotions.

Now reflect on the teachings of the sages who say that what you're looking for is what you already are, that it's not something you need to cultivate or find; it's your natural state, and you've never been apart from it even for an instant. Right now, let go of your search and abide as awareness or presence itself.

Don't try to figure out what this means or meditate in your accustomed way. Just trust that you merely need to let go and be. Rest in the peace and joy of your essential nature. Gaze out at the world through the eyes of unconditional, nonjudgmental presence. This silent presence is what's looking through these eyes right now, and nothing the mind says can make it otherwise. Even concepts like "peace" and "joy," "unconditional" and "nonjudgmental," are superfluous and misleading. Just be who you are!

Continue to remain as you are as you get up and go about your day.

3

FREEDOM FROM THE KNOWN

The fact remains, all knowledge is a form of ignorance.
The most accurate map is still only paper.

—*Nisargadatta Maharaj*

As a young child, I had an insatiable curiosity about the world around me. I collected insects and flowers and spent long hours wandering through the forest near my home, merged with my surroundings in a timeless dimension of beauty and light. In school, this curiosity found expression in a fascination with books and ideas, and my teachers were soon praising my ability to solve complex problems and remember significant facts. Gradually, I began to take pride in my accomplishments and to identify myself as a brainy kid, an intellectual. In sixth grade, I emblazoned on my notebook the motto "Knowledge is power."

By the time I reached college, I began to realize that all my conceptual knowledge didn't have the power to deliver the one thing I wanted most: happiness, peace of mind, ease of being. Some of the brightest people I knew were miserable. One, a brilliant mathematician, jumped to his death from his dorm room, and another, one of my closest friends, overdosed on psychedelics and ended up in a mental hospital. My professors, considered among the best in their field, were visibly dissatisfied with their lives and, from all I could tell, had no connection with a deeper source of meaning and knowing. They could talk for hours about *King Lear* or the Bhagavad Gita, but they appeared to know nothing about their own hearts and souls.

NOT KNOWING IS THE MOST INTIMATE

Fortunately, I had already begun exploring the wisdom of the East, particularly Zen, where the sharp sword of discernment cuts through conditioned beliefs to reveal the living truth beneath. Longing to transcend the burden of my busy mind and the pain of a difficult childhood, I finally put aside my Zen books and began practicing meditation. Instead of studying other people's ideas about life, I became intimate with life itself—cleaning houses, preparing food, working in the garden, following my breath, teaching others how to meditate.

Ten years later, as the head monk in a monastery in California, I was asked to select a koan for the Dharma dialogue that marked the end of my tenure, and my choice reflected a profound transformation in my attitude toward knowing:

Zen Master Dizang saw his student Fayan dressed in traveling clothes and asked him, "Where are you going?"

"Around on pilgrimage," Fayan answered.

"What is the purpose of your pilgrimage?" asked Dizang.

Fayan said, "I don't know."

"Ah," replied Dizang, "Not knowing is the most intimate."

Not knowing is the most intimate. Concepts of any kind only serve to separate you from the rich, intimate, juicy experience of this moment right now. Once you label the flower or the insect, psychoanalyze your partner or friend, break your body down into its component muscles and bones, you no longer really see them as they are, but only as the mind understands them to be, trapped in an intellectual framework that freezes the river of constant change into a single frame and leaves out the flow that makes the river what it is. This conceptual overlay separates you from life and leaves you feeling estranged and disconnected. To paraphrase John Lennon, life is what's happening while you're busy imposing your interpretation on it.

But if you set aside your ideas, you have the potential in each moment to experience life directly, intimately, without any division between knower and known. Sensing your body from the inside, without the interference of the mind, gives you an opportunity to step through a doorway into a direct apperception of being itself—pure, radiant, undivided—where subject and object are one. As the mystic and poet William Blake put it, "If the doors of perception were cleansed, everything would appear to man as it is, infinite." Even Saint Paul understood this truth when he wrote, "For now we see through a glass, darkly [that is, a mind clouded by concepts], but then face-to-face: now I know in part; but then shall I know even as also I am known." In other words, in spiri-

Breathe and Reflect

As you did at the end of Chapter 1, take a few moments to gaze around the room as if you were an infant encountering the world for the first time. You don't know what anything is or what it's called, you're just aware of shapes, colors, movement, the play of light and dark. Set aside any concepts or beliefs that may arise, and continue your innocent looking, free from conceptual overlay. How does this looking affect you?

tual illumination, the apparent separation between knower and known dissolves into pure, undivided knowing, which is simply existence itself.

Pretending that you know deprives you of the intimacy of your true nature, which is as near to you as your own skin. In fact, the truth of your being can never be known by the mind—it's elusive and ungraspable—but as soon as you completely let go of your struggle to know, the truth reveals itself to you. "You must unlearn everything," says Nisargadatta Maharaj. "God is the end of all desire and knowledge."

The world's scriptures are filled with sayings that warn against the limitations of conceptual knowledge and point to the ineffability and unknowability of the Divine. Yet these teachings have not stopped the great religions from amassing countless volumes of conceptual elaboration on the most fundamental spiritual truths. Even Buddhism, which emphasizes the importance of direct spiritual experience, often comes replete with centuries of encrusted beliefs that burden the seeker with a clouded lens through which to interpret the path. One of my students, for example, got involved with a Tibetan Buddhist sect that taught that enlightenment was possible if she devoted herself to her teacher and engaged in rigorous practices. The promise of awakening lured her on, but the more committed she became, the more she was exposed to other, more disturbing teachings that warned of the fires of painful hell realms if she in any way violated her vows to her guru. By the time she came to me, she was having nightmares about going to hell and was terrified she would end up there—simply because she had wanted to wake up to her essential nature.

NO SWEETS FOR THE EGO

The Jewish tradition tells a wonderful story about the dangers of taking even the most exalted religious doctrines too seriously. One day, it seems, the founder of the Chassidim, Israel the Baal Shem Tov (Master of the Good Name), was experiencing an elevation of his soul in the heavenly realms, as he was accustomed to do. There he met Satan, the angel responsible for bringing challenging situations to Earth, gesticulating and reading aloud from a book. From Satan's words and gestures, the Baal Shem could tell that the book contained a version of his own Torah teachings.

When he returned to his body, he called together his close disciples and asked who among them had written a book of the Baal Shem Tov's Torah. Sure enough, one of the disciples sheepishly came forward, holding a small journal in which he had carefully recorded the teachings he had personally heard from the master's lips. The Baal Shem Tov read the book, then handed it back to the student and said, "Not a single statement in this book is true." By this, the Baal Shem did not mean that the concepts were inaccurate, but that the words no longer carried the wisdom of their source—they were dead, lifeless replicas, without the power to evoke the Divine.

Too bad the Buddha can't return like the Baal Shem to read the volumes of admonitions and theories that have been propounded in his name and declare them distorted, inaccurate, outdated, and inert. Every Buddhist sect and school makes different claims about what the Buddha really taught, but the truth is that the so-called words of the Buddha recorded in the Pali canon were written down more than five hundred years after the master's death. Can you remember what you said last month, last week, or even yesterday? How, then, can the "words of the Buddha" be reliably transmitted for five centuries from one generation of monks to another without alteration? Who knows what the Buddha really taught? Yet millions of men and women revere these words as the gospel according to Buddhism and live their lives in alignment with them.

In his wisdom, the Baal Shem realized that Satan, the tempter, could take words that were meant merely as pointers to divine revelation and fashion them into a golden calf, a false idol to be worshipped in place of the living truth that must arise anew in each individual heart. In the same way, the mind takes possession of even the highest spiritual teachings and pretends to know the truth of which they speak, whereas the mind is merely seeing reality through the cloudy lens of spiritual concepts.

No doubt you know people who have read all the right spiritual books and imbibed the most refined spiritual concepts and can repeat them verbatim, but have no direct experience of the truth behind the words. These people identify with—and believe themselves to be sanctified by—the spiritual knowledge they've accumulated but still suffer and cause suffering as if nothing has changed. Perhaps you've used spiritual concepts in the same way.

The spiritual marketplace is filled with well-intentioned folks who collect teachings the way some people collect antiques and take comfort and pride in admiring them. The first time I met my teacher Jean Klein, I described the teachings I had studied and the books I'd read, and he smiled lovingly and said softly, "Put down your baggage." Jean called such concepts "sweets for the ego" because they give the mind a false sense of power and control over what simply cannot be controlled or known, a feeling of solid ground where no ground exists. Such concepts interfere with your ability to awaken because they give you the mistaken impression that you already know.

Of course, religions develop in the same way, beginning with a genuine, vital spiritual revelation that gets passed from generation to generation and gradually loses its juice as fewer and fewer disciples experience the simple, radiant truth behind the words. Over time, the religion degenerates from living communion to rigid dogma, from the sayings of the masters infused with the power of their source to a collection of dead words that are enshrined in holy books and scriptures, defended against apostates and nonbelievers, and worshipped from afar as the sacred and irrefutable pronouncements of the enlightened or divinely inspired ones of old.

RADICAL SPIRITUALITY

Radical spirituality takes an entirely different approach. Instead of offering more beliefs for your collection, it slashes away at your most cherished assumptions to reveal the root, the living source, from which all concepts spring. "Throw it away!" says Nisargadatta Maharaj. "Whatever you understand is not the truth and is to be thrown overboard." Indeed, radical spirituality teaches that your ideas and stories are the only things that separate you from the truth of your essential nature. Once you stop taking them as reality and see them for what they are, mere thoughts, you have an opportunity to fall back into the vast, spacious, luminous, thought-free presence that is always already who you really are—the living reality that no thought can possibly touch. "Realization is not the acquisition of anything new or a new faculty," says Ramana Maharshi. "It is only the removal of all camouflage."

Buddhist masters and Indian sages aren't the only ones to emphasize letting go of conceptual baggage, as the story of the Baal Shem Tov makes clear. Christian mystics like Meister Eckhart and Saint John of the Cross expounded what later came to be known as the *via negativa* (the way of negation), which teaches that nothing you can say about God is true, because God is a vast emptiness beyond all conceptual knowing. "God the ineffable one has no name," wrote Eckhart, adding that "the highest and loftiest thing that you can let go of is to let go of God for the sake of God"—that is, the concept God for the living God. Yet according to the masters of the via negativa, you can know God directly and indisputably, beyond the mind.

Jesus himself said, "It's easier for a camel to pass through the eye of a needle than for a rich man to enter the kingdom of heaven." Although he was primarily talking about an attachment to material wealth, he was also referring metaphorically to the wealth of beliefs by which many people in his day (and ours) identified themselves: Pharisee, Sadducee, liberal, conservative, Muslim, Jew. "You must become as little children to enter the kingdom of heaven," Jesus preached in the Sermon on the Mount—meaning you must be innocent, open, receptive, with childlike faith unencumbered by dogma. The path that Jesus taught emphasized spiritual poverty and humility, stripping yourself bare of the old in order to be baptized and reborn in the newness of the Now.

THE LURE OF FUNDAMENTALISM

Spiritual dogma can be extremely seductive, despite the admonitions from the various spiritual traditions to avoid succumbing to its temptations. Through your spiritual beliefs, you can gain a sense of security and comfort in a world that may otherwise seem threatening or chaotic, create community with other like-minded people, organize your life according to certain fundamental principles, and connect with a current of spiritual energy that has been transmitted from one generation to the next. In the process, however, you trade the possibility of experiencing reality directly for a familiar, reassuring, unquestioned (and unquestionable) filter that you project onto the real. Such filters in turn make up the spiritual ideologies and dogmas that wreak so much havoc in the world. (By the way, I'm not suggesting that there's anything wrong with spiritual beliefs per se. In fact, some of them are masterful creations of the human imagination, like poems or symphonies. The suffering begins only when you become attached to them and mistake them for truth.)

Recently, I responded to a flyer announcing a gospel music festival near my home in Austin, Texas. After I arrived, I quickly realized that I had stumbled on a revival meeting in disguise, and that the audience was a relatively close-knit group of evangelical Christians who regularly convened for music and prayer. The people I met were friendly and kind, and the singing was filled with heartfelt love and devotion. In my ecumenical way, I found myself grooving on the good vibrations as I translated the references to Jesus into more generic references to the Divine. Soon, however, the performers began interspersing their songs with hostile comments directed at those who didn't share their conservative political views. The love and devotion never stopped flowing, but now it was being filtered through layers of judgments and beliefs. If you didn't believe in old-fashioned family values, support the Republican Party, and above all put your faith in Jesus, you were undeserving of love and destined for damnation.

More than their judgment of others, though, what struck me about these lovely, heartful men and women was how judgmental they were of themselves. Considering the commentary that accompanied their songs, they seemed to be struggling mightily to be good Christians and resist the temptations of Satan because they believed that they were inherently flawed and unworthy and that their natural insights and impulses were misguided. Their faith provided them with the possibility of salvation, but it also kept them bound by their sinfulness. I could understand why they held so tightly to their religious beliefs. Without the reassurances such beliefs provided, they might have to face the uncertainty and self-doubt they were trying to overcome.

FILLING THE VOID WITH BELIEFS

Fundamentalists aren't the only ones who feel inadequate and attempt to compensate by adopting the right attitudes and beliefs. As a psychotherapist, I've found that just about everyone I've counseled believes at some level that he or she is inadequate or unworthy, and many approaches to therapy attempt to bolster people's self-esteem by substituting positive beliefs for negative ones. The problem is that no amount of bolstering will ever completely reassure the ego, the apparently separate self, that it's adequate because it knows at some level that it's just a construct, a collection of thoughts, memories, and feelings, without any substantial existence. In the words of Ramana Maharshi, the ego is just a "shadow cast on the ground" by being. No wonder it feels inadequate—it doesn't really exist!

Developmentally, the ego arises in childhood when you're given the message that you're not enough just as you are and that you need to act in certain ways to win love and ensure your survival. For example, your parents may tell you, with the best of intentions, that good girls don't get angry, they're cheerful and accommodating, or that big boys don't cry, they hold their feelings in and tough it out. Then they give you positive attention when you act in certain acceptable ways. As a result, you start pretending that you're happy or strong even when you don't genuinely feel like it, and a split develops between your inner experience, which is deemed unacceptable, and your outer persona, or ego. If you're like most folks, you may spend the rest of your life attempting to win love and approval or ensure your survival by pretending to be someone you're not, while deep down feeling inadequate because you never succeed at living up to the image you project for yourself.

There's nothing wrong with this process—indeed, it appears to be unavoidable—but it can cause quite a bit of suffering. Many people, for example, turn to addictive behaviors in a futile attempt to fill the hole or vacancy they sense inside themselves with alcohol, drugs, antidepressants, food, sex, material possessions, and, yes, spiritual beliefs. The inner emptiness can seem so terrifying and overwhelming that they'll do just about anything, including indulging in self-destructive behaviors, to avoid facing it.

Spiritual beliefs provide the ego with a more positive identity to layer on top of the hole and compensate for the feelings of inadequacy. "I must be a good person," you may think, "because I follow the words of the Gospels, the teachings of the yogic sages, the sayings of the Buddha." Over time, you fashion these beliefs into a comforting inner world with a more exalted, more spiritual you at the center, but this world is just a fantasy, another construct, more sweets for the ego, and it won't bring you any closer to genuine spiritual awakening.

Breathe and Reflect

Even this book is filled with words and concepts that can be confusing or misleading. Don't take them seriously or try to hold on to them. Just let the words resonate inside you, then throw them away. My deepest wish is that you put down this book knowing less than when you picked it up. The process of unknowing is the path to wisdom.

Radical spirituality burns down the walls of your fantasy world and invites you to face your feelings of lack and inadequacy directly, without conceptual overlays. In the light of present awareness, you come to see that the separate self is just a construct and the feelings are just that—merely feelings—and have nothing to do with who you really are, which is the limitless space in which thoughts and feelings arise. "Give up the tendency to define yourself," says Nisargadatta Maharaj. "Whatever concept you have about yourself cannot be true." Indeed, the feeling of inner emptiness, which may seem so threatening, actually points to the radiant emptiness or void at the heart of existence. As you penetrate the many layers of belief and self-concept, you may feel moved to ask the deeper questions that can lead you to a direct experience of this radiant void: What is life really about? What's the point? Who am I really? (For an in-depth exploration of self-inquiry, see Chapter 5.)

Even the most spiritually correct, nondual concepts can be co-opted by the ego and turned into a comfortable spiritual identity. I know people who regularly attend spiritual gatherings and retreats, read the works of the Zen masters and Advaita sages, speak nondual jargon, and spout the philosophy ("I am consciousness. There's no division between self and other. The separate self doesn't really exist."). But they're merely repeating dead words rather than expressing their realization, and the ideas and beliefs to which they're so attached just hinder clear seeing and may ultimately act as obstacles to awakening. As Nisargadatta says, "The most accurate map is still only paper."

At an even subtler level, despite the words to the contrary, the emphasis on conceptual knowing just reinforces the seeming solidity of the knower, the separate someone who thinks it knows. "Cease to be a knower," says Ramana Maharshi. "Then there is perfection." I often tell my students that I hope they'll leave my talks and intensives knowing less than when they came, and I encourage them to forget the words and let the truth behind the words continue to resonate inside them, beneath the level of the mind.

CRITIQUING THE NEW AGE

In any discussion of spiritual beliefs, the New Age deserves special mention for its tendency to take fundamental spiritual truths and enlist them in the service of the spiritual ego. Read an author like Deepak Chopra, for example, and you'll find the most profound spiritual principles articulated with utmost clarity—until you get to the part about how you can use the techniques and teachings he espouses to increase your wealth and maximize your longevity. Suddenly the nondual teachings have been turned into a treatise on self-improvement, which is fine if what you're looking for is a better, healthier, wealthier you.

Not long ago, friends and clients were urging me to watch a movie called *The Secret*, in which a series of New Age teachers bears witness to the power of a metaphysical principle known as the "law of attraction"—essentially, the belief that you create your own reality through your thoughts, feelings, and expectations. According to this principle, which is central to New Age philosophy, if you envision wealth, health, and happiness, not only with your mind but with your whole being, the universe will cooperate, and you'll inevitably get what you want.

The problem is that life doesn't necessarily work that way, except in the broadest of outlines. Yes, it's true that if you act loving and generous, for example, you'll tend to attract love and generosity in return. But will you inevitably get the Porsche, the big house with the pool, or the ideal mate just by wanting them intensely enough, as several of the presenters suggest? It doesn't appear to be so. There are simply too many factors involved in life's unfolding on the material plane, most of them well beyond your control: genetics; family circumstances; physical limitations; karma from past lifetimes; issues of race, gender, and socioeconomic status. I watched one of my spiritual teachers die a painful death from stomach cancer, another drown in a pond while attempting to save his young daughter, and a beautiful awakened friend succumb to brain cancer just a few days shy of her forty-second birthday. Had these deeply spiritual beings merited such difficult or untimely deaths by doing something wrong or thinking the wrong thoughts?

Some New Age teachers would contend that they could have prevented or at least forestalled their deaths by envisioning good health, but this argument raises the issue of New Age guilt. If you create your own reality, the argument goes, then you must be to blame if you're suffering. Following this line of reasoning to its logical conclusion, you're left with the belief that all those who are poor, hurt, sick, or lonely have failed to envision a better life for themselves with enough clarity and heart, which is patently absurd.

Besides, who really knows what's best for you? Although you may hunger for the big house, the fancy car, and the successful career, there's inevitably a vaster, more complex, and more mysterious order at work that the human mind can't comprehend—and that may not include the results you desire. "If you want to make God laugh," the old saying goes, "tell her your plans." When the virtuous, prosperous, devoutly religious Job loses everything he's cherished—his wealth, his health, his children—and laments his losses to God, complaining that he doesn't deserve his fate, God appears to him in a whirlwind and reveals the unfathomable immensity and profundity of the Divine. Job is so overwhelmed and humbled by this vision that he falls to his knees in awe and supplication. "Do you think you know what's best?" God seems to be saying. "What hubris! Only I have the omnipotence and the omniscience to make the heart beat and the planets spin in their orbits, to give and take away, to create and destroy."

You may want to substitute *consciousness, being, Tao,* or *Buddha nature* for *God,* but the point is still the same: the little me you take yourself to be doesn't really know what's best for you and has only very limited control over the circumstances of your life. The point of spiritual awakening is not to maximize your assets and minimize your losses, but to be free of attachment to gain or loss and to be peaceful and joyful in the midst of whatever life brings.

Perhaps the deepest question raised by the belief in the law of attraction is "Who is the you who supposedly creates your reality?" When you awaken to your true nature, you can say with utmost confidence that you're the source of your own reality—not you as the limited body-mind, but you as the vastness of being, the Tao, the current of life, which is constantly creating and destroying in its own mysterious and unpredictable way. At this stage, you come to realize that you want exactly what life brings, because you're not separate from life and not attached to having it any other way.

THE VALUE OF KNOWING

Needless to say, in the relative world of cause and effect, certain kinds of knowledge are invaluable. If, for example, you're a doctor, lawyer, teacher, computer programmer, or mechanic, you need to have access to a vast reservoir of information to do your job properly. If you want to answer e-mail or surf the Web, you need to know enough about computers to get you there. By contrast, conceptual knowledge won't reveal to you who you are, but it may help orient you in your search.

Jean Klein used to say that conceptual understanding can afford you a "geometrical representation" of truth, by which he meant an accurate road map of the territory, a clear pointer to the truth beyond concepts. Ultimately, however, this map can take you only so far—to the threshold of realization but no further, to the precipice over which you must fall in order to awaken—and then you must be "taken" by the truth itself in a moment out of time. When you awaken, your conceptual understanding dissolves in "being understanding," the living, nonconceptual knowing of the heart.

Ramana Maharshi puts it simply: The teachings are like a stick used to stir a fire and keep it burning. Once the fire is raging and needs no tending, you can throw the stick into the flames and let it burn as well. So books like this one have some value if they ignite the fire of truth in your heart and help keep it ablaze. In the end, however, you need to let go of all concepts, even the most accurate ones, and die into the deepening wisdom of the heart.

**What's the difference between not knowing
and mental confusion or dullness? Sometimes
my meditations seem to go by in a flash and I
can't remember a single moment, as if I've been
lost in a fog.**

The not knowing I refer to is not confused or dull at all; it's clear and bright, aware and awake to what is, without any conceptual overlay to cloud the experience. Not knowing is a limitless spaciousness beyond the mind, whereas confusion and dullness are merely passing mental states. When you sit, be alert and present for what is, including the mind-states that come and go. By the way, your sitting may also seem to pass quickly when you're one with what you're experiencing and there's no separate little me to keep track.

**I feel like I identify more with my feelings than
with my thoughts or beliefs. How does this radical
approach to spirituality apply to me?**

If you identify with your feelings, they act as a filter (just as beliefs do) that separates you from a direct, unmediated experience of life. In certain circles, feelings are given more credence than thoughts, but most feelings are based on conditioned reactive patterns we learned as children and on deeply held beliefs about how life should (or shouldn't) be. If you feel so inclined, you might try to unearth the ideas and stories beneath your feelings. In any case, not knowing means seeing life clearly, free from both emotional and conceptual filters. Of course, feelings come and go spontaneously like thoughts and needn't be a problem if you don't identify with them.

I worry that I'll have no moral compass to guide my actions if I abandon all of my spiritual beliefs. Don't our ethical principles keep us from acting in a completely selfish way?

On a relative, everyday level, ethical principles can be helpful in guiding our actions and maintaining social order. But the spiritual beliefs on which they're based tend to cause more suffering in the long run because they divide "us" from "them," the good from the evil, the saved from the damned, and set up an ongoing argument with the way things are. Even the most benevolent, exalted beliefs just separate us from the mystery of life as it is. The more you set aside your beliefs and encounter life directly, without argument or struggle, the more you discover a natural responsiveness that's inherently gentle, loving, and ethical and doesn't require a spiritual worldview to maintain. Of course, if you're attached to your spiritual beliefs, I have no intention of separating you from them. I just invite you to examine them closely and see how they affect you.

Wake-Up Call

Who Would You Be Without Your Spiritual Beliefs?

Set aside fifteen to twenty minutes for this exploration. Make a list of your most cherished spiritual beliefs. At first, you may have difficulty identifying them because you don't consider them beliefs, but rather the truth. However, any view or interpretation of reality you can formulate in words, no matter how true it may seem, is just a belief and open to question.

Now take each of the five most significant beliefs and begin to inquire:

- Can I really know that this belief is true?
- How does attaching to this belief affect me?
- How do I act toward others when I hold this belief? How do I act toward myself?
- How do I feel in my body? Do I feel lighter, freer, more spacious? Do I feel heavier, denser, more constricted?
- What am I afraid of experiencing or feeling that this belief protects me from? (Perhaps it's an inner feeling of emptiness or lack or a fear of the unknown.)
- How does this belief contribute to a spiritual identity I've constructed for myself?
- Who would I be without this belief? What would my life be like, how would I feel, and how would I act toward myself and others?

Ask these questions for each belief in turn, and notice how the answers affect you.

4

THE PRACTICE OF PRESENCE

In your absence is your presence.

—*Jean Klein*

*I*n my early days as a Zen student, I had the opportunity to spend time with three exceptional teachers: Shunryu Suzuki, one of the first Zen masters to teach in the West; Kobun Chino, who helped Suzuki Roshi establish monastic practice at Tassajara Zen Mountain Center near Big Sur; and the Tibetan teacher Chogyam Trungpa, who founded the first Buddhist university in the West. These three masters taught as much through the power of their silent presence as through their words, and each was a renegade in his fashion, open to adapting traditional forms to the needs of contemporary Western students. From Kobun especially, I received the mandate, which I pass on to my own students today, to find my own way and not be bound by tradition. "Never call yourself a Buddhist," he often said.

One afternoon Kobun and Trungpa, who were good friends and accomplished calligraphers, met in a friend's living room to drink tea and share their brushwork, with several of Kobun's students in attendance. As one teacher looked on, the other spread out a large piece of paper, knelt down, gracefully stroked some words of spiritual wisdom (Trungpa in Tibetan, Kobun in Japanese), and then translated what he had written. After a pause, the other teacher did the same. Before long, the exchange became a kind of playful Dharma combat, the ritualized doctrinal debates common to both Zen and Tibetan Buddhism, with each man responding to what the other had written.

At one point Trungpa, who was dressed in his customary suit and tie, leaned over and inscribed the phrase "Mindfulness is the way of all the buddhas," emphasizing the cornerstone of traditional Buddhist practice—moment-to-moment mindful awareness. Kobun, with the billowy sleeves of his monk's robes tucked under his arms, picked up a large brush, saturated it with black ink, paused, and then wrote with a mischievous flourish, "Great no mind." Everyone in the room broke out in uproarious laughter.

In addition to being a classic example of the brotherly one-upsmanship so common in Zen stories, this exchange points to two fundamentally different attitudes to spiritual unfolding. According to the traditional Buddhist view, you need to practice mindful awareness of each moment with great dedication and diligence, gradually developing the penetrating insight necessary to see through the illusion of a separate self. In the process, you're expected to cultivate positive qualities like patience and compassion and minimize or eliminate undesirable emotions like anger and fear. Gradually, with enough mindfulness meditation and the cultivation of enough virtue, you transform yourself into a buddha.

But from the perspective of the direct approach often (though not always) encountered in Zen, you're already a buddha just as you are, and meditation is an opportunity to express your limitless, radiant, innate Buddha nature—what Kobun referred to as "great no mind." (By the way, Kobun and Trungpa were not polarized on this issue but shared a mutual appreciation of both perspectives.) The distinction finds expression in countless koans and stories. Consider, for example, the following from China's Tang dynasty: When Master Nan-chuan saw his student Ma-tsu diligently practicing meditation hour after hour, he could sense a certain ambition and end-gaining in the young monk's demeanor, so he sneaked up behind him and asked, "What are you doing?"

"I'm trying to become a buddha," Ma-tsu replied proudly.

Nan-chuan then picked up a stone and began rubbing it against a spare tile from the monastery floor.

Hearing the sound, Ma-tsu asked, "What are you doing?"

Said Nan-chuan, "I'm trying to make a mirror."

As often happens in such stories, Ma-tsu had an awakening. Just as a tile is what it is, not a mirror in the making, you are already just what you've always been, and you don't need to practice to become it.

THE LIMITATIONS OF MINDFULNESS

The exchange between Kobun and Trungpa also points to two very different approaches to working with the mind. In the practice of mindfulness—which is quite popular these days in the West not only as a spiritual path, but also as a secular technique for reducing stress and enhancing well-being—you pay careful, deliberate attention to your experience as it changes and unfolds from moment to moment; it's sometimes described as a cat tracking a mouse or a mother attending to her newborn child. After months and years of regular practice, the mind becomes accustomed to releasing its preoccupation with past and future and centering itself in the experience of the now.

But attending to the particulars of experience in this way runs the risk of becoming effortful and laborious and, as its name implies, strengthening the illusion of the separate self that's looking down on reality from a distance, trying to be mindful. In fact, being mindful ("mind-full") can just energize the localization of energy and attention in the witnessing mind and accentuate the gap between subject and object, self and other, that awakening is intended to close. The mind may become proficient at paying attention and fancy itself an accomplished meditator. In reality, however, true meditation, which has nothing to do with the mind, is always occurring and merely needs to be allowed, not created.

After spending years on my cushion efforting to be mindful of my breath, I eventually developed the capacity to sit with unwavering focus for hours at a time, but my sitting was lifeless and dry, like a withered branch. No sign of insight, awakening, or spontaneity in any direction. "In the beginner's mind, there are many possibilities," Suzuki Roshi said. "In the expert's mind, there are few." In the process of becoming an expert meditator, my mind had gradually become more rigid and narrow, and I'd lost the innocence, openness, and aliveness of beginner's mind, which had delighted and nourished me in my early days of practice.

During one particular retreat, I can remember exerting my usual concentrated effort to pay attention and suddenly finding the whole process so amusing that I burst out laughing. Here was my mind, busily struggling to meditate, and all the while I was being embraced by a silence so deep I could feel it in my bones. The meditative habits of a lifetime fell away like an old skin, revealing the raw

Breathe and Reflect

Begin by sitting quietly for a few moments. Now open your awareness wide and welcome whatever arises without judgment or resistance. Don't try to control or manipulate your experience in any way, just let everything to be as it is. You're relaxed yet alert, present but not fixated in any way. You may be completely unfamiliar with this way of experiencing reality. Spend a few minutes sitting in silent presence. Notice how it affects you.

immediacy of the moment. I didn't need to meditate; meditation was always happening, I just needed to let go and join it. There was no place to go, nothing to do, no more tricks up my sleeve, just the indivisible and ineffable Now. At last, my mind had given up trying, if only for an instant, and I had happened upon the doorway to true meditation.

When I finally awakened to my essential nature, I looked back and realized that the innocent, open awareness with which I had begun my practice was in fact identical with the expansive, all-inclusive awareness that had subsequently awakened to itself through me. Indeed, this one undivided awareness was the natural state toward which all meditation points, the profound silence I had stumbled upon during retreat. It was not something I could possibly fabricate or develop, but the very consciousness that had always been looking through these eyes and hearing through these ears. Yet I had taken an extremely circuitous path to discovering it, spending years cultivating mindfulness in order to reveal the "great no mind" that had paradoxically never been absent even for an instant.

THE PRACTICE OF PRESENCE

As I ultimately discovered, the mind can't possibly meditate, though it may manage a good imitation. In its ongoing struggle to remain in control, the mind will read the books and become adept at the practices, ironically succeeding at "quieting" itself. But in the end, the states that the mind creates or achieves—the stillness, the peace, the compassion, the insight—are just forms of mental activity and have nothing to do with the true peace and stillness of your essential nature, which is beyond the mind and can only be revealed, never developed. "You are awareness," said the Indian sage Ramana Maharshi. "Awareness is another name for you. Since you are awareness, there's no need to attain or cultivate it." In other words, you are the welcoming space in which reality reveals itself. Without this awareness, nothing would exist.

As an alternative to paying mindful attention to your breathing and other particulars of your sensate experience, I recommend a different approach, both in sitting meditation and in everyday life: the practice of presence. Instead of focusing the light of your awareness like a laser on a particular object or activity, you open it like the sky, welcoming the experiences that arise just as the sky welcomes the clouds, neither ignoring nor indulging them. Instead of concentrating, you relax and let go, allowing everything to be just as it is, without any attempt to control on your part. You're alert but at ease, totally present but not fixated in any way. As Ramana suggests, you can't fabricate presence because it is what you are; you can only step aside and let it happen. Any effort is an indication that your mind has intervened. You may find this practice confusing and uncomfortable at first, because your mind is more accustomed to concentrating and holding on, which anchors it securely in the realm of the known, than to relaxing and letting go, which opens it to the unfamiliar and possibly frightening prospect of the unknown.

My Advaita teacher Jean Klein, who was a classically trained violinist, likened presence to the function of listening. When you listen, your awareness is naturally global, expansive, and receptive; the mind doesn't tend to focus or fixate on sounds the way it does on visual objects, but rather opens to what is without picking and choosing. "Just open to the openness," Jean was fond of saying. This quality of complete openness and receptivity is of the same nature as consciousness itself, which welcomes what is without resistance or preferences. Eventually, presence ceases being a practice, something you do, and naturally dissolves in consciousness, unconditional presence, without a separate someone being present. "It is like being alone in the desert," said Jean. "At first, you listen to the absence of sounds and call it silence. Then suddenly you may be taken by the presence of stillness where you are one with listening itself." The realization that the separate someone doesn't exist marks the ultimate fruition of the practice of presence. "In your absence is your presence," Jean often observed.

Of course, the Buddhist practice of mindfulness is intended to lead to the same realization, but it can instead reinforce the subtle control of the mind. One friend, a long-time Zen student and a teacher of the Alexander technique (a refined approach to posture and breathing), recently suggested that the original purpose of the core Buddhist practice, mindfulness of the breath, was to bring you to the point where you let go and realize that you don't breathe, you're actually breathed—that is, there's only breathing, with no separate someone breathing. In the words of Suzuki Roshi, the "I" is "just a swinging door that moves when we inhale and when we exhale." In reality, however, the practice of mindfulness often turns into a kind of contest to see how "mindful" the separate someone can be.

TO MEDITATE OR NOT TO MEDITATE

Throughout the history of the direct approach, including the traditions of Zen, Dzogchen, and Advaita Vedanta, people have argued about the relative merits of meditation. At one end of the spectrum are those who insist that you're already a perfect expression of your radiant, essential nature just as you are, and any deliberate attempt to meditate separates you from what you've always been, reinforcing the illusion of a goal to be achieved and a someone who meditates. At the other end are those who contend that, even though you're perfect and complete just as you are, you need to meditate to realize this fact. (For more on this paradox, see Chapter 1.) Nowadays, many hardcore Advaitists believe that practices of any kind are antithetical to realization because they constellate a doer that doesn't really exist. By contrast, many devoted Zen practitioners consider regular meditation practice to be a prerequisite for enlightenment.

Perhaps the most famous expression of this age-old debate can be found in the story of the Sixth Patriarch of Chinese Zen, Hui-neng. Originally an illiterate woodcutter from the southern frontier, Hui-neng was enlightened as a young man even before entering the monastery when he heard these words from the Diamond Sutra: "Cultivate a mind that dwells nowhere." Recognized immediately for his extraordinary clarity by the Fifth Patriarch, the young novice nevertheless toiled away in the monastery kitchen, gathering firewood and washing pots, because his teacher didn't want to upset the monastery hierarchy by acknowledging him. Eventually, the Fifth Patriarch invited his disciples to submit their understanding in the form of a poem, hoping that this contest would help reveal his true successor. The head monk wrote the following verse and posted it on the monastery wall:

> Our body is the bodhi tree,
> Our mind is a mirror bright.
> Carefully we wipe them, hour by hour,
> And let no dust alight.

The meaning here is that we need to meditate regularly in order to clear our minds of the negative emotions and habitual patterns that obscure our true nature.

When the young Hui-neng heard this verse being repeated by one of the monks, he knew the realization it expressed was incomplete and had someone write the following rejoinder:

> There is no bodhi tree,
> No stand of a mirror bright.
> Since everything is empty,
> Where can the dust alight?

In other words, your true nature is inherently empty and pure and can't be obscured even for an instant; therefore, what need could there possibly be for meditation? Needless to say, this verse was approved by the Fifth Patriarch, and he secretly appointed Hui-neng his successor.

Of course, many teachers embrace both points of view, contending paradoxically that the secret of your true nature may be open, but it's still a secret until you make it your own. "The Tao is basically perfect and all-pervasive. How could it depend on practice and realization?" wrote Zen Master Eihei Dogen more than seven hundred years ago. Yet as long as your mind is confused by attachments and preferences, he advised, you need to take "the backward step that turns your light inward to illuminate the Self" through the practice of meditation.

According to the twentieth-century Indian sage Ramana Maharshi, the Self alone exists, and separate objects are merely the illusory play of consciousness. From this perspective, there's nothing to practice and nowhere to go. "Transcend what, and by whom?" he often said. "You alone exist." Yet Ramana also recognized that most people suffer because they don't realize who they are, and he taught a variety of practices depending on the needs and maturity of the seekers. Some, he believed, could benefit from sitting in silence and practicing self-inquiry, whereas others might be better suited to prayer or mantra recitation. For those rare few who were already poised on the threshold of awakening, he simply offered the direct pointer of his words and the profound silence of his presence.

Jean Klein counseled his students not to make meditation a habit, but rather to allow the genuine silence that is ever-present behind the noise of everyday life to increasingly draw them to itself: "When you become responsive to the solicitations of silence, you may be called to explore the invitation." Otherwise, meditation merely evokes a temporary state of mind, a kind of enforced tranquillity that inevitably ends when your meditation comes to a close, rather than the abiding silence that has no beginning or end. Jean likened meditation to a laboratory that you enter when silence solicits you, for the sole purpose of discovering the meditator. Deliberate attempts to meditate regularly just

Breathe and Reflect

When you put down this book and go about your day, let yourself be solicited by silence. When your mind pauses for no apparent reason, consciously merge with the silence between the thoughts and allow the silence to expand, rather than efforting to fill your mind again. When you sense the presence of this silence, which is always available beneath all the noise, stop what you're doing for a moment and enjoy it.

create expectations of future results and reinforce the fictitious identity of the meditator. When you finally recognize that the meditator is merely a figment of the imagination fabricated from thoughts, feelings, images, and memories, you no longer need to experiment—awakening has become your ongoing reality.

For my part, I would echo the advice of Nisargadatta Maharaj: "Do it if you're doing it, and don't do it if you're not doing it." If you're drawn to sit quietly, then honor the impulse, and if you have no interest in meditation, then don't feel obliged. In any case, don't meditate because you think you should, and pay attention to the beliefs and stories the mind produces to explain the path you've chosen. The fact is, the separate meditator arises as a function of the stories you tell yourself about meditation—for example, "Now I've got it, I'm really doing well," or "I have no idea how to meditate, I'll never become awakened," or even "I don't need to practice anymore, I'm beyond that." In the end, your attachment to these stories is the only thing separating you from true meditation, the profound silence beneath all the words. "Realization is already there," says Ramana Maharshi. "All that is necessary is to get rid of the thought 'I have not realized.'" Such thoughts and stories rise and fall like waves on the mysterious and unfathomable ocean of the Self. There's no need to get rid of them. Just see them for what they are and—whether or not you choose to meditate—fall in!

SETTLE THE SELF ON THE SELF

As you may have noticed, I use the term *meditation* to refer both to the deliberate practice of sitting quietly and being present for what is and to the natural state of unconditional awareness or presence that is always already occurring. Ultimately, if your sitting is free of artifice and effort, the one dissolves into the other, the gap between subject and object disappears, and only presence remains. This undivided, nondual presence is your natural state; it's always available right here and now, and many teachers over the centuries have found that relaxed, effortless, silent sitting seems to be uniquely suited to opening you to the possibility of awakening to it.

Such sitting is actually quite simple, in the sense of being uncomplicated, but it's definitely not easy, primarily because the mind likes to complicate even the simplest activities. In fact, "just sitting," as it's known in Zen, is considered the most advanced and refined practice in the Buddhist tradition precisely because it's so simple. Even though I describe this practice in some detail in the section on presence and provide guidance in the "Wake-Up Call" at the end of this chapter,

I thought it might be helpful to include some illuminating words of instruction from several teachers and texts that have moved me over the years. As you read these words, along with my commentary, notice which ones resonate most deeply for you. In the end, they're pointing to exactly the same place.

• **"Cultivate the mind that dwells nowhere."** (**Diamond Sutra**) One of the clearest descriptions of unconditional presence, these famous words from a Buddhist text highly esteemed in Zen self-destruct as you read them. The phrase could just as easily read "No cultivation, no mind, no dwelling, nowhere." Just this! When the mind doesn't dwell or fixate, reality is free to be itself, and suffering and resistance come to an end. The result is true meditation.

• **"Settle the self on the self with imperturbability."** (**Dainin Katagiri**) These words from one of my preceptors when I was a monk make no sense to the rational mind, but they invite a deep, silent, unshakable sitting. In fact, when the self settles on the self, the self disappears, and reality blossoms just as it is. In his own meditation practice, Katagiri Roshi exemplified the truth of these words.

• **"No thought, no analysis, no reflection, no intention, no cultivation. Let it settle itself."** (**Tilopa**) Instead of teaching technique, this great Tibetan master instructs through negation, essentially admonishing you not to do any of the usual mind manipulations common in the meditation of his day (and ours), but rather to get out of the way and let meditation happen. The mind naturally settles down if you let it, just as the sediment in a pond eventually falls to the bottom if you stop disturbing the water.

- **"All you have to do is find out your source and take up your headquarters there."** (**Nisargadatta Maharaj**) This is easier said than done, of course. Finding out your source is tantamount to awakening to who you really are. But once you catch a glimpse of your source, abide there as much as possible, not only when you meditate, but throughout the day. Live your understanding from moment to moment, advised Jean Klein. Serve the truth that you've realized, counsels Adyashanti.

- **"In true meditation, the emphasis is on being awareness—not on being aware of objects, but on resting as primordial awareness itself."** (**Adyashanti**) As you relax and let everything be just as it is, the tendency for awareness to fixate on objects naturally relaxes as well, and awareness spontaneously becomes aware of itself. True meditation is a kind of homecoming—you recognize the place immediately, and every cell and fiber of your being lets go and relaxes in relief.

THE ENERGETICS OF MEDITATION

Although it may seem abstract, the practice of presence is actually quite sensate and involves wholehearted attention to bodily experience. In fact, the clear perception of what is, unclouded by conceptual overlay, provides a powerful portal to the eternal Now, as Eckhart Tolle observes. To repeat the words of the English mystic and poet William Blake, "If the doors of perception were cleansed, everything would appear to man as it is, infinite."

As awareness clarifies and naturally settles on itself, noticeable energetic and physical experiences may occur. The locus of your awareness (the place your awareness tends to come to rest) may shift from your forehead (home of the neocortex) to the back of your head, and then to the lower part of your body, usually either your heart or tantien (the center of gravity two inches below your navel). You may find that you increasingly act from your heart and move from your gut, rather than from your thinking mind. You may also experience rushes of energy up your spine (kundalini) or more subtle, extremely pleasurable vibrations throughout your body (bliss). As you sit quietly, you may notice thoughts and feelings passing through and releasing without leaving any residue of heaviness or discomfort. Above all, you may gradually discover that your inner experience no longer has the same hold over you, no longer causes the same stress and contraction, and you feel lighter, more spacious, more peaceful, more loving, yet at the same time more disengaged.

Be careful, however, not to interpret these energetic experiences as meaning more than they actually do. They are just experiences and don't necessarily signify that spiritual awakening has occurred. Be aware also that genuine energetic experiences of this kind can't be fabricated; they can only be allowed as an expression of the natural unfolding of presence.

In the end, meditation is supremely simple: just sit down and let everything be as it is. Any attempt to manipulate or calm the mind or make meditation happen just interferes with your natural state of true meditation. "Remain as you are, without question or doubt; that's your natural state," said Ramana Maharshi. These wise words speak for themselves, though it's crucial to remember that the you he's talking about includes everything, without exception. Ultimately, "you alone exist."

**You offer a pointed critique of mindfulness
practice. But can't it prepare the ground for
the practice of presence?**

Perhaps, though I wonder why any ground needs to be prepared. Just be present for what is. It's quite direct and requires no preparation.

**But how can I work with my mind and
get it to settle down?**

The idea that the mind needs to calm down is just another spiritual belief put forward by the progressive approach to meditation. It's a diversionary tactic designed by the mind, which loves to do battle with itself. Try as hard as you can, you'll never get the mind to settle down. Indeed, all your efforts to calm it just make it more agitated. Rather, let the mind do what it does, and rest as the primordial awareness that isn't disturbed by the perturbations of the mind.

The mind's nature is to move, but you are not your mind; you're limitless, silent, ungraspable presence. Paradoxically, of course, when you leave the mind alone, it tends to calm down by itself.

My mind just runs my life. It's busy all the time and gives me no rest.

You don't suffer because your mind is so active, you suffer because you identify with the drama it creates and take it to be the truth of who you are. Instead of struggling with your mind, become aware of the beliefs and stories it churns out and then inquire into their validity, as I describe in the "Wake-Up Call" at the end of Chapter 3.

How can I tell the difference between being "invited" to sit in meditation, as you put it, and sitting because I think I should?

There will be moments in daily life when your mind spontaneously stops and an empty space or gap opens up. In this space, you have an intimation of a stillness and silence beyond the mind. Instead of immediately rushing to fill the gap in your effort to stay busy, let the silence and stillness solicit you. Enjoy these empty, unfurnished moments and gently allow them to expand. This is how you're invited to meditate.

By contrast, when you look at your watch and say, "Oh, it's time for my daily sitting"—or even more to the point, when you decide that your mind is too busy and you need to do something to calm it down—you're meditating because you think you should. When you have the thought, "I should meditate now," ask yourself, "What is missing from my experience that I think meditation would provide?" Then ask, "Do I really need to go off to find it, or is it available right here and now?"

Wake-Up Call

The Practice of Listening

Set aside ten to fifteen minutes for this exploration. Begin by sitting comfortably with your eyes closed. If possible, sit in or near a natural place like a garden or park, or at least a space where you hear only background sounds like the hum of a refrigerator, the rumble of traffic, or the sounds of birds. Make sure you're not going to be disturbed by voices, music, radios, or TVs.

Now open your awareness to the sounds around you. Don't focus on any particular sound or jump from sound to sound, just open your awareness like the lens of a camera and listen to the play of sound with your whole body, not just your ears. Allow listening to happen. The sounds come and go, shift and change, in this expanded, global awareness. Everything is happening in you.

Keep relaxing, letting go, and allowing listening to happen. If your awareness habitually focuses or jumps from sound to sound, just let it do what it does as you continue to relax in global awareness. You may find that you naturally include other sensations as well: the contact of your body against the chair, the air against your skin, the rumbling of your stomach, the beating of your heart. Just keep allowing the play of what is, without efforting to pay attention in any way.

Eventually, the sense of a separate experiencer may drop away, and only experiencing remains. No separation between subject and object—just this!

As you continue allowing experiencing to happen, you may discover that it arises in a limitless stillness and silence that can't be experienced in any way. This is your very own Self, unconditional presence, consciousness without a second, the source of all experience. You can never know it with the mind; you can only be it knowingly.

Allow everything to be as it is as you relax into the silent presence that you've always been.

5

WHO IS EXPERIENCING THIS MOMENT RIGHT NOW?

Before Abraham was, I am.
—*Jesus of Nazareth*

As you become more relaxed, open, and present for what is, with less resistance and struggle, you may find at times that the sense of a separate self becomes lighter and more attenuated, or even disappears entirely. The one who is apparently doing the work of being present dissolves into unconditional presence, in which awareness and the objects of awareness are one. No longer is there someone watching and something being watched, there's just this single, seamless, nondual reality—just this. The Chinese poet Li Po describes it this way: "We sit together, the mountain and me, until only the mountain remains." Simultaneously, you may experience a profound silence and stillness that underlies everything and seems more authentic and real than the thoughts and feelings you generally take yourself to be.

Such glimpses constitute a preliminary awakening to your timeless spiritual nature and may whet your appetite for deeper and clearer revelation. Indeed, the continued practice of presence, which at a certain point becomes natural and effortless, may ultimately flower into a complete recognition of who you are, in which awareness becomes aware of itself as the limitless, ungraspable silence, openness, and space in which everything arises. Or you may happen upon awakening quite unexpectedly, without practicing or seeking in any way. Often, however, the process of awakening involves some form of deliberate self-inquiry, some intentional attempt to find out who you are.

INVESTIGATING THE SEPARATE SELF

Even if the sense of a separate self—what Ramana Maharshi called the "I-thought"—drops away from time to time, it tends to be extraordinarily tenacious and continues to assert its control over your life until you discover once and for all that it's not who you really are. You may have experienced gaps in the illusion of a substantial, continuous self, but you haven't realized that the space and openness that reveals itself in these gaps is your true nature. Instead, you keep returning to your habitual, default identity as the body, mind, and personality. Until awareness awakens to itself, this openness remains merely a curious spiritual experience and never flowers into the truth of your being.

After all, you've spent your entire life identifying with a particular set of characteristics, emotions, memories, and beliefs and a particular life history. No wonder this identity feels so natural and goes unquestioned. The people in your life reinforce this identity and join you in the consensus view that you're a separate someone in a world populated by other separate someones who interact and coexist. The

I-thought lays claim to every experience and action and makes them seem personal and centered right here, in this body-mind called me. But radical spirituality introduces the possibility that the separate someone is not the true center but merely a construct, another wave on the surface of the ocean of being, and the practice of presence may offer you a glimpse of this ocean, this deeper reality. The next step is self-inquiry.

In self-inquiry, you have an opportunity to turn the light of your awareness from your outer affairs to your inner experience and investigate the separate self. Does it actually exist as a consistent, ongoing entity, or is it merely an assemblage of thoughts, feelings, memories, and images? And if it's just an assemblage, a construct, then who are you really? In self-inquiry, you generally start out looking for what you are but end up encountering everything you're not—your body, your sensate experiences, your thoughts, your emotions—until you find yourself on the outer margins of the known, at the precipice of the unknown. Once the mind exhausts itself in the search, which is the purpose of self-inquiry, you're available to be taken by the realization of what you are, not as another thought or experience, but as a living reality. The point of self-inquiry is not intellectual analysis or understanding, but direct pointing beyond the mind to the truth of your being, which can never be known by the mind.

For the purpose of this discussion, I've divided self-inquiry into three different currents, or forms: spontaneous, formal, and turning words. These are just conceptual distinctions designed to placate the mind, which loves to divide and describe. In reality, there are as many forms of self-inquiry as there are individuals, and any genuine attempt to discover who you really are can be effective if you undertake it wholeheartedly.

Spontaneous Self-Inquiry

When you fully realize that what you're seeking doesn't exist in manifestation and can't be found "out there" in experiences or states of any kind, there's a relaxation of being and a cessation of seeking. This is true renunciation, not as asceticism or denial, but because you see that complete fulfillment is only available in the Now. Once this is finally acknowledged by the mind, there is a giving up, and attention naturally turns back on itself in a kind of spontaneous self-inquiry. Such sudden moments of giving up the search can serve as powerful pointers to the source of all seeking, which may reveal itself in an instant, without effort or practice.

Of course, spontaneous self-inquiry may also be just the beginning of a prolonged investigation that ultimately includes other forms of self-exploration. One of my students, for example, describes how he first began to inquire during a snowball fight when he was a child. Every time the other boys would hit him with a snowball, they would shout, "I got you, I got you," but he would shout back, "No, you didn't get me. You only got my arm or my leg or my head." At some point, he realized that no matter where they hit his body, they never managed to hit *him*. The mystery of this paradox caught his attention, and he found himself wondering, "Who is this me that can't be hurt?" Thus began a lifetime of self-inquiry that ultimately led him to the study of Advaita Vedanta.

My own initiation into the practice of self-inquiry occurred one day as a teenager when I gazed into the mirror and felt the presence of a watcher who seemed to be separate from me. "Who's watching?" I wondered with a frisson of fear. For months afterward, I couldn't look at my reflection without a rush of adrenaline, but my curiosity was piqued, and several years later, I began practicing Zen.

Breathe and Reflect

Spend some time paying attention to your body. Look at your arm or your leg or feel your head or face, and consider that they belong to you but aren't who you are. Even your heart or your brain is "yours" but not the essence of you. The natural next step is to ask, "Then who am I really?"

Formal Self-Inquiry: Who Am I?

Perhaps the best-known approach to self-inquiry is also the most direct—the practice of asking the question "Who am I?" Popularized by the twentieth-century Indian sage Ramana Maharshi and his successors, this question naturally turns awareness back on itself in an attempt to discover the one who is aware. As human beings, we use the term "I" repeatedly, as if we know what it means, but who, what, and where is this "I"? You say, "I see," "I think," "I do," "I want," but to what does this "I" refer? You give this "I" ultimate power and value in your life and go to great lengths to fulfill its needs or defend it against attack. But do you really know what it is?

For the practice of self-inquiry to be effective, you need to recognize at some level that the word "I," though superficially referring to the body and mind, actually points to something much deeper—or, perhaps more accurately, to nothing at all. Anything you can perceive, no matter how intimate—including the physical body and the cluster of images, memories, thoughts, feelings, and beliefs that constitute the mind—is merely an object of perception; it can't possibly be the perceiver, the "I" in "I notice, I think, I feel." But who is this perceiver, this experiencer, the ultimate subject of all objects? This is the real question at the heart of "Who am I?"

Instead of "Who (or what) am I?" you may prefer asking, "Who is thinking this thought? Who is feeling this feeling? Who is seeing through these eyes right now?" The point of these questions is not to engage the mind, because the mind inevitably gnaws on questions endlessly like a dog on a bone, with little nutritional benefit. Instead, drop the question into the stillness of your being like a pebble dropped into a still forest pool. Let it send ripples through your meditation, but don't attempt to figure it out. When the pool is relatively tranquil again, drop another pebble and see what happens. (By *tranquil*, I don't necessarily mean "absent of thoughts.") Set aside any conceptual answers, such as "I am the Buddha," "I am consciousness," or "I am a spiritual being of light," and come back to the question. Though true at a certain level, these answers won't satisfy your hunger for spiritual sustenance any more than a painting of chocolate can satisfy your longing for sweets. As you continue your self-inquiry, you may find that the question begins to catch fire, and you notice yourself asking it not only during meditation, but at unexpected times throughout the day. "If the mind is distracted, ask the question promptly, 'To whom do these distracting thoughts arise?' " counsels Ramana Maharshi.

Let your inquiry be fervent and wholehearted, but not obsessive or effortful, and don't let it become automatic or habitual, like taking your vitamins because you've been told they're good for you. Similarly, the inquiry can only be fruitful if it's grounded in the bodily experience of welcoming presence; otherwise, it may just exacerbate the sense of separation and disembodiment. "Without this welcoming openness, this global feeling and sensitivity, the question 'Who am I?' remains intellectual," says Jean Klein. "If it is ever to become a living question, it must be transposed on every level of our being. The openness in the living question is the doorway to the living answer." The more you genuinely want to know who you are and the deeper you keep looking, beyond the answers churned out by the mind, the more likely the question will one day reveal the answer, not as a particular thought or experience, but as the timeless, unchanging ground of all experience.

As an alternative to asking "Who am I?" you might follow Ramana Maharshi's advice to focus your attention on the subjective feeling of "I" or "I am" behind your experiences until the experiences themselves, the objects of thought and awareness, fade into the background and only the "I" remains. If you can sustain this awareness of "I," the individual I-thought will dissolve into a direct experience of the Self. " 'I am' is the goal and the final reality," Ramana said. "To hold it with effort is inquiry. When spontaneous and natural, it's realization."

Like any practice, self-inquiry runs the risk of becoming progressive if you view it as a gradual path to some distant goal. Remember that you're not trying to develop, manipulate, or cultivate any particular mind-states in order to arrive somewhere or become something you are not already. Instead, ask the question and allow a response to emerge right now, then let it go. The question may keep recurring, but resist the temptation to make a "practice" out of it.

Formal Self-Inquiry: Koan Practice

Though more enigmatic and elusive than the straightforward question "Who am I?" the Zen stories and riddles known as koans lead to the same realization by tying the mind in knots and forcing it to let go so the truth can emerge from beneath the undergrowth of thoughts. Foundational koans like *mu* and "original face" are designed to awaken you to your innate Buddha nature, while more advanced koans invite you to express your Buddha nature in a variety of situations. Generally, formal koan practice only makes sense under the direct guidance of a teacher who has already solved the koans.

One of the best-known foundational koans, "What was your original face before your parents were born?" stops the mind in its tracks and immediately shifts the inquiry from the familiar realm of the known to the dimension of the unknown—and possibly unknowable. After all, the person you take yourself to be didn't exist before the birth of your parents, so what face could the koan possibly have in mind? In fact, on present evidence, you can't even say that you were ever born—the birth of the body-mind is just a story, a memory in the mind of your parents (or not even that), and the birth of who you really are is merely a convenient fiction that has no reference point. Clearly, your original face is identical to the "I" in "Who am I?" and you can engage this koan in exactly the same way.

In the progressive approach of the Rinzai school of Zen, the koan *mu* is posed as the formidable barrier through which every student must pass in order to achieve kensho. (The full koan goes like this: A monk asked Zen Master Chao-chou, "Does the dog have Buddha nature?" Chao-chou replied, "*Mu* [no].") I can still remember sitting retreats in which every participant was required to bellow, "*Mu*," while the head monk prowled the meditation hall with a long stick, smacking students on the shoulders and shouting, "Die on your cushion" to encourage them to wake up.

The problem with this approach is that awakening rarely happens as the result of such concentrated effort—in fact, it doesn't seem to happen as the "result" of anything at all—and relaxation generally seems more conducive to realization than tension and struggle. Besides, different koans or questions resonate for different folks, and no cookie-cutter approach works for everyone. Recently, I counseled a woman who had been practicing Rinzai Zen for many years

and felt deeply ashamed and inadequate because she hadn't
succeeded in passing *mu*. As we talked, it became clear that
the koan made no sense to her and didn't elicit any genuine
interest or curiosity, but she kept practicing it because her
teacher required it. When I encouraged her to find a question that really appealed to her, rather than banging her
head fruitlessly against the same old wall, she was so grateful
and relieved that she started to cry.

My first Zen teacher, Kobun Chino, always encouraged his students to formulate the living question that was
uniquely their own, and the great Japanese Zen master Eihei
Dogen emphasized embracing the koans that everyday life
presents. Indeed, life is constantly affording opportunities to
discover not only who you are, but also how you can express
who you are in every activity. The questions that grab you
and ignite your passion for truth inevitably prove to be the
most potent in evoking self-realization. For example, losing a mother or father early in life may awaken in you the
penetrating question "Who dies?" Or experiencing intense
physical pain may prompt you to investigate the question
"Where is the peace beyond pleasure and pain?" Everyday
koans like these have the power to lead directly to the recognition of true self, which is beyond pain and death.

Formal Self-Inquiry: Unfindability

The approach to self-inquiry known as "unfindability" is
exemplified in the famous exchange between the founder
of Chinese Zen, Bodhidharma, and the Confucian scholar
Hui-k'o. While sitting quietly gazing at the wall of the cave

where he spent nine years in meditation, Bodhidharma was approached by Hui-k'o, who earnestly sought his instruction. "I have not yet found peace of mind," Hui-k'o said. "Please pacify my mind for me."

"Bring me your mind, and I will pacify it for you," Bodhidharma replied.

Hui-k'o spent weeks in fervent self-inquiry, attempting to find his mind so he could take it to his teacher, but to no avail. At last, he went to Bodhidharma and said, "I have looked for my mind everywhere, but I've been unable to find it."

"Ah," said Bodhidharma. "Then I've succeeded in pacifying your mind for you."

At this, Hui-k'o was enlightened. In other words, no matter how carefully he searched, Hui-k'o could not grasp the entity called mind, because such a substantial, separate mind (or self) simply doesn't exist. Recognizing the essential emptiness and nonlocatability of mind, Hui-k'o finally awakened to the truth of his being.

The Tibetan Buddhist tradition known as Mahamudra ("great seal"), which I had the good fortune to practice under the guidance of several teachers, goes one step further by recommending that students ask a series of specific questions about mind and self that reveal their inherent unfindability. For example, I might ask you to examine the objects you call "mine" and find the so-called me to whom they belong. But no matter how hard you look, you won't be able find it, because the body and mind are also "mine" and therefore can't be the me to which "mine" refers. Or I might ask

Breathe and Reflect

Where do you suppose your thoughts arise? If you say, "In my head," then try to locate them. Where exactly does thought occur? How big are your thoughts? What color, shape, and density? They seem to have so much reality, but can you point to them or describe them with any degree of accuracy? What happens to your thoughts when you try to describe them?

you to sit quietly in meditation and then attempt to locate the mind and determine its density, shape, color, and form. But no matter how earnestly you try, you won't be able to answer these questions.

"Not finding anything, you may initially think that you have somehow failed," explains Tibetan master Thrangu Rinpoche. "Either you misunderstood how to look, or you just haven't looked enough. But in fact, this is not true. The reason you find nothing . . . when you look for your mind, is that the nature of your mind is utter insubstantiality, emptiness. We need to experience this directly in meditation."

Turning Words

"Live with the sayings of the teacher and the reminders of truth these awaken," my teacher Jean Klein used to say. "These unspoken reminders are the perfume of that to which they refer" and may naturally guide the listener back to their source. Even without formal self-inquiry, the essential teachings of the great masters and sages can precipitate an awakening in the student who is poised on the precipice of truth. The Zen tradition uses the term *turning words* for the pithy phrases that spontaneously turn the student's mind toward true nature. Often completely incomprehensible to the mind, these phrases are regarded as "live words" (as opposed to the "dead words" of conceptual discourse) and constitute the beating heart of many koans. (A disciple asked Zen Master Tung-shan, "What is Buddha?" The master responded, "Three pounds of flax." When a student asked Zen Master Yun-men the same question, his answer was equally inexplicable: "A piece of toilet paper.") Likewise, Tibetan teachers often use verbal "pointing-out instructions" similar to the turning words of Zen to point their students directly to the nature of mind.

But turning words often work their magic independent of koans or formal pointing-out instructions and may arise in any situation. As a monk, I was never particularly adept at formal koan practice, but my teacher Jean Klein was a master of spontaneous turning words, and his formulations would often shock my mind into silence and spontaneous self-inquiry. For example, I can still remember one particularly intense retreat in which he responded to a friend's question with the following pronouncement: "Even though your body and mind have changed dramatically since childhood, you've always used the word 'I' to refer to yourself. What is this 'I,' the one who has experienced your life from infancy until today, through all the changes, but has itself remained unchanged?" Essentially, Jean was asking, "Who are you?" but the evocative way he described the unchanging witness—and my openness and receptivity to his teachings—allowed his words to resonate and ripple deep inside me the way a formal koan had never been able to do.

During another retreat, Jean periodically repeated the statement, "The seeker *is* the sought; the looker *is* what he or she is looking for," in a slow, hypnotic voice, with an emphasis on the word *is*. Each time something inside me would vibrate, like a tuning fork resonating to a familiar frequency. At the end of the retreat, as I was driving home, not thinking of anything in particular, the phrase "The seeker is the sought" floated up into consciousness like a bubble. Suddenly my entire world turned inside out, and I knew without doubt exactly what those words meant.

Even if you don't have a living teacher, you have access to the written wisdom of the great masters and sages and can allow their words to resonate inside you in the same way. The key is to sit quietly, set aside your conceptual filters and interpretations, and let the teachings drop into the still pool of your being like pebbles. Choose sayings that seem enigmatic or paradoxical but also somehow inviting to you, and don't make any attempt to understand them at a conceptual level, though conceptual understanding may gradually present itself. Just live with the ripples, the silence and forefeeling of truth that these sayings evoke. Eventually they may awaken you to the living source from which they arose.

Throughout this book I offer formulations that may act as turning words if you're ready. Here are a few more that have had particular resonance for me:

The eye with which I see God is the same eye
with which God sees me.

—*Meister Eckhart*

You are the light behind all perceptions.

—*Jean Klein*

God is a circle whose center is everywhere and
whose circumference is nowhere.

—*Empedocles (also attributed to Pascal)*

You have not understood until you have
solved the riddle of the one who thinks he has
understood.

—*Nisargadatta Maharaj*

Consciousness and its objects are one.

—*Jean Klein*

SILENT TRANSMISSION

Perhaps even more awakening than the live words spoken
by an enlightened sage is the silence in which he or she
abides—or, more accurately, the silence that he or she is,
fundamentally. The ultimate source of all the nondual teachings, this silence has the power to draw the listener more
and more deeply into itself—into the fertile emptiness from
which manifest reality springs—and to elicit in those who
are ready and oriented a direct experience of truth. Without
this silence as ground, even the most profound pronouncements are nothing but empty talk.

Ramana Maharshi spent much of his time in silence and would often respond to questions by gazing silently into the eyes of the questioner and only then responding briefly in words. Neither a strategy nor a teaching technique, Ramana's silence was the natural expression of his deep abiding as the undivided Self of all. Jean Klein, who similarly taught through silent presence as well as words, often said, "In your absence is your presence." Indeed, when the separate self is entirely absent, as it is with sages like Ramana or Jean, the silent presence is powerful and all-pervasive.

In the Indian tradition, seekers may travel long distances simply to sit in the presence of an enlightened master or sage. Known as *darshan* ("seeing"), the silent, mutual gazing that occurs is considered to be the source of tremendous blessing and even spiritual illumination. But silent presence can never cause awakening, any more than the parting of the clouds can cause the radiance of the sun. Rather, the limiting and confusing patterns and beliefs (*samskaras*, or *vasanas*) naturally burn up in the light of the Self like clouds before the sun, revealing the innate luminosity that all beings share.

In the Zen tradition, the passing of the Dharma ("truth") and the mantle of teacher from master to disciple involves what Bodhidharma called a "special transmission outside the scriptures, no dependence on words or letters," but a "direct pointing to the human heart" (meaning true self, or the nature of mind). In fact, the Zen lineage traces itself back to one of the Buddha's primary disciples, who reportedly received transmission when the Buddha silently held up a flower, and the disciple, Mahakasyapa, simply smiled.

PRESENCE AND INQUIRY

Remember that inquiry only bears fruit in a heart that is open and available for truth. Being present for what is just the way it is (as described in Chapter 4), which naturally flowers into unconditional presence or listening, calms the pool of mind without effort or manipulation and allows the pebbles of inquiry to spread their ripples throughout your welcoming awareness. Instead of "practicing" presence, you might prefer following Adyashanti's instruction to "rest as primordial awareness itself," if these words resonate for you. But deliberate practices aren't always necessary. Sometimes the rawness of suffering or crisis or the loss of a familiar identity or ground may blow you wide open, stop your mind, and invite spontaneous self-inquiry. Like Job, you may even have the good fortune to find yourself stripped of everything you hold dear and pleading with God for a voice from the whirlwind to reveal to your tear-filled eyes the truth of your existence. In such moments, only the absolute truth will suffice.

**The question "Who am I?" just stimulates
my thinking. What should I do?**

Don't ask the question like a mantra that you repeat automatically again and again. Instead, reserve it for moments when you feel open and aware and relatively stress-free. Then ask yourself the question slowly several times. Let it resonate throughout your whole being, and allow an answer to emerge—or not. Above all, don't try to figure it out with the mind—you won't get any answers worth having.

You may find it helpful to remind yourself that you use the word "I" constantly to refer to some inner point of reference, as in "I see, I hear, I feel." But this "I" doesn't refer to the body or the mind, since both of these can be experienced. So who is this "I"?

If you still find that the question "Who am I?" activates your mind, you can use an alternative, such as "What am I?" or "What is this?" or "Who is experiencing this moment right now?" (described in detail in the "Wake-Up Call" at the end of this chapter). If none of these questions appeals to you, feel free to formulate one that does or set aside self-inquiry entirely. Remember that no technique or practice is required to awaken to the truth of who you are.

When I ask the question "Who am I?" or "Who or what is aware right now?" all that comes is "I don't know." I feel like I'm not doing it right.

"I don't know" is a wonderful answer. It means that the mind has given up trying to formulate a conceptual response and finds itself on the edge of the unknown. Let this not knowing be vivid and alive, rather than dull or resigned. You're alert, present, aware, and you don't know who you are. Keep looking for the "I," and let the not knowing resonate.

Isn't it enough to "be still," as Ramana Maharshi suggests? What's the point of activating the mind with questions when I'm already resting in silence?

If you're truly resting not only *in* silence, but *as* silence, then all questions are unnecessary. Generally, however, there's a subtle separation between the "I" who's resting and the silence in which it rests, which is implicit in the words you use. You can spend days and even years resting in this way without genuinely awakening to the vibrant truth of your being. Self-inquiry, which Ramana himself heartily recommended, is designed to collapse the gap and allow the separate self to dissolve completely in the silent ocean of the Self.

Wake-Up Call

Who Is Experiencing This Moment Right Now?

Set aside twenty to thirty minutes for this exploration. Begin by sitting quietly with your eyes closed for five minutes or so. Rest your awareness on the experience of sitting, and allow your body to relax.

Now open your eyes and allow your awareness to settle on a particular object: a table, a chair, a bookcase, a desk. As you gaze at this object, ask yourself, "Who is seeing?" Clearly, the object is seen, but who or what is seeing? If you reply, "I am, I'm the one who's seeing," ask yourself further, "Who is this 'I,' and where is it located?"

Next, open your awareness to the sounds around you. Clearly, sounds are being heard, but who or what is hearing? Again, you may say, "I am, of course," but who is this "I," and where is it located?

Set aside any conceptual answers, such as "I am consciousness" or "I am a child of God or a being of light," because they won't provide the answer you seek. Relax, breathe softly, and let your inquiry be direct and experiential. "Who am I? Who am I really?"

Perhaps, like many people, you believe that you are your brain or your thoughts. But both of these can be experienced—you can sense your brain and think your thoughts. The deeper question is "Who is sensing and thinking?" Likewise, if you point to your heart, consider that your heart and your feelings also can be experienced. But who or what is experiencing? Anything you can locate or name is an object of awareness. The question is "Who is aware? Who is the ultimate subject of all objects?"

Keep inquiring, in an ever-deepening regression, trying to find your way back to the "I," the source of all experiencing. If your inquiry becomes too effortful or mental, just relax and sit quietly once again. After a few minutes, resume your questioning, not as an intellectual exercise, but as a whole-body search for the ultimate experiencer. You say, "I feel, I think, I see, I taste, I know," but who is this "I"? Who is experiencing this moment right now?

6

SPONTANEOUS AWAKENING

Transcend what, and by whom? You alone exist.
—*Ramana Maharshi*

*O*ne day, Tony Parsons was walking across a London park when his attention spontaneously shifted from his thinking and his preoccupation with future events to the feel and pressure of his footsteps as he walked. After a few moments, quite unexpectedly, the me watching the walking dropped away and only the walking remained. "Total stillness and presence seemed to descend over everything," he recalls in his book *As It Is*. "All and everything became timeless, and I no longer existed. I vanished and there was no longer an experiencer."

For Parsons, who did not have a meditation practice or a spiritual discipline, this experience without an experiencer occurred as an unexpected and unsolicited revelation and quickly blossomed into a full-blown spiritual awakening. "Oneness with all and everything was what happened," he writes, "and an overwhelming love filled everything." He had stumbled on what he called an open secret, "an apparent gift that had always been available and always would be"—the fact that "nature, people, birth and death, and our struggles, our fears and our desires are all contained within and reflect unconditional love."

For Suzanne Segal, the awakening occurred unexpectedly as well. Devoted to the practice of Transcendental Meditation in her early twenties, Segal, a Chicago native, had stopped meditating, married, and moved to Paris with her French husband. Pregnant with their first child, she was stepping onto a bus one warm afternoon when her accustomed sense of identity "was forcefully pushed out of its usual location inside me into a new location that was approximately a foot behind and to the left of my head. 'I' was now behind my body, looking out at the world without using my body's eyes," she relates in her memoir *Collision with the Infinite*.

For Segal, this sudden shift in identity came not as a blissful spiritual realization, but as a shocking loss of something comfortable and familiar, which she spent years trying to recapture. Only after she met a spiritual teacher who confirmed her discomforting experience as a genuine spiritual awakening was she able to relax and allow it to flower into the full recognition that she was not only nothing, but everything.

As a child growing up in New York City, Robert Adams found that he had a magical power—he could get whatever he wished for by repeating God's name three times. One day, at the age of fourteen, he sat down to take a math test and applied his technique as usual to provide himself with the correct answers. Instead, he had a powerful, spiritual illumination in which the world lost its substantiality, and everywhere he looked he could see only the unchanging Self, the all-penetrating, all-prevailing source of existence. "There was no time, there was no space, there was just the 'I am,'" he recalls in *Silence of the Heart*. "Everything was the 'I.' The word 'I' encompassed the whole universe, and a limitless, indescribable love permeated everything."

Needless to say, the young Adams was irrevocably transformed by what he had so unexpectedly experienced and immediately lost interest in his usual studies, hobbies, and friends. After several years spent searching for someone to help him understand what had happened, he eventually found his way to India, where he studied for three years with the great sage Ramana Maharshi. "It was with Ramana that my eyes were opened to the meaning of my experience," Adams says.

My own initial awakening, which occurred while I was driving on a California freeway, was not as dramatic or as unanticipated as Adams's or Segal's, but it still had the power to turn my accustomed way of seeing myself inside out in an instant. Instead of being centered in the body-mind, where I had thought I resided, I suddenly realized that I was actually this global luminosity, this awake, aware space in which the body-mind and everything else appeared—and this "globality," this "one bright pearl" (as Zen Master Hsuan-sha called it), was the only reality, timeless and ever-present. The words "There's no going away from it" kept running through my head as waves of bliss coursed through my body.

THE NATURE OF AWAKENING

These revealing stories, not of Indian sages or Zen monastics but of ordinary Westerners, demonstrate the often spontaneous, disconcerting, and life-transforming nature of genuine spiritual awakening. In a moment out of time, your accustomed identity crumbles, and you see beyond the veil of conventional reality to the deeper spiritual ground or undercurrent of existence, of which the material world is merely a manifestation. As a consequence, you can never again view your life in quite the same way, as if it were ultimately real, permanent, or substantial.

The term *awakening* is so appropriate and so often used because most people actually do have the sense of waking up from the dream they previously took to be reality—of being a solid, separate someone in a world of other solid someones—and realizing that this seeming reality is merely a translucent, evanescent appearance floating on the surface of a deeper reality, like a bubble on a pond or a wave on the ocean.

Of course, you may have preliminary glimpses of your true nature in which the sense of a separate experiencer drops away momentarily but quickly returns and reestablishes its control, or brief moments of groundlessness in which you enter the mysterious current of life but quickly resurface as a separate self. Authentic awakening, however, generally involves a powerful figure-ground shift in identity that radically and permanently transforms your experience of reality. Once you awaken, you can never completely go back to sleep, though you may doze off from time to time; once you know who you are, you can never completely forget, though the knowing may seem to disappear or elude you.

Every genuine awakening has its unique particulars, as the stories told here show. Some take place as a gentle homecoming, a final recognition of what you've always known yourself to be. Some, like Suzanne Segal's, occur as a sudden, forceful stripping of the veil that separates you from some vaster reality. Others, like Tony Parsons's, penetrate through the illusion of a separate self in an instant, like a sharp sword cutting through layers of encrusted beliefs, revealing the living truth at the core. Still others resemble a gradual dissolution, like ice melting into water and merging with the sea. Some awakenings are dramatic and filled with powerful imagery or energetic experiences; others are almost entirely uneventful, like slipping quietly down a rabbit hole—or perhaps a birth canal—into a completely new world.

Breathe and Reflect

Spend some time noting the ideas and preconceptions you have about spiritual awakening. Where did these ideas originate? How do they influence your attitude toward spirituality? Once you've identified these ideas, set them aside, and open yourself to the possibility of genuine awakening.

THE INTERSECTION OF TIME WITH THE ETERNAL

Whatever the particulars, spiritual awakening occurs at the intersection of the vertical and horizontal dimensions of being. As Westerners, we move through life almost exclusively on the horizontal plane of time and space, carrying the baggage of our beliefs and our personal history, working diligently to achieve certain goals while being fearful of failure, loneliness, and death. Like everyone else we know, we take ourselves to be separate individuals bound to the roller-coaster ride of pleasure and pain, fulfillment and suffering, health and sickness, which eventually ends in old age and death.

But each moment offers us an opportunity to awaken to another dimension in which time and space no longer apply and everything radiates unconditional presence and the timeless divinity of being. Sometimes called the eternal Now, this vertical dimension is always infusing and informing the horizontal and inviting us to awaken to our spiritual nature. Indeed, every moment is already the intersection of the time-bound and the timeless, form and the formless, the horizontal and the vertical. Like Jesus, whose cross symbolizes this intersection, you are both a human being and God simultaneously—you just need to recognize this truth. Though meditation and self-inquiry may invite this recognition, it occurs just as often without preparation, spontaneously and unexpectedly, as an inexplicable gift.

THE INITIAL PHASE OF AWAKENING

Despite the differences among awakening experiences, there appears to be a commonly applicable movement or unfolding to the awakening process. In the initial awakening, you generally find that the locus of your identity is dislodged from your usual sense of self and shifted, either gently or forcefully, to the uninvolved witness who is always aware but never a part of what it witnesses. You may experience this witness as a vast spaciousness, a profound silence or stillness, a deeper ground underlying all things, or (as in Suzanne Segal's case) a disembodied reference point that eventually dissolves and never reappears. More than a mental insight or epiphany, this shift is an energetic, whole-body change in the location and content of who you take yourself to be. Rather than localizing yourself in the brain, where most Westerners believe the "I" exists, you now recognize that thoughts, images, feelings, and memories actually arise in a timeless, boundaryless space—and this space is your true identity, the "I" you genuinely are. (In Zen this limitless spaciousness and nonlocatability is known as emptiness, or the absolute.)

Needless to say, such a sudden shift may be disconcerting, as Suzanne Segal's story attests. Sometimes it's accompanied by powerful energetic releases or by deep feelings of wonder, gratitude, love, or relief. In my own case, waves of ecstatic energy flowed up my spine and out the top of my head like a fountain for hours. Just as often, especially if you're not spiritually inclined or schooled in the phenomenon of awakening, it may prove frightening or overwhelming. For years after her initial awakening, Segal would feel a rush of panic whenever she looked in the mirror and couldn't identify the face she saw there, and my own bliss soon began alternating with fear as my mind struggled to regain control from an energy that seemed to be threatening to overwhelm and destroy it. Eventually, however, most people get used to their new, expanded identity and glean from the detachment it brings a peace and equanimity that are not so easily disturbed by the ups and downs of life.

THE FULL FLOWERING OF AWAKENING

As transformative as it may be, the shift in identity from the personal, psychological self, which is composed of thoughts and feelings and localized in the head, to the formless, non-locatable emptiness that contains and pervades everything is only the first stage in the full flowering of awakening. Although the realization that everything, including the separate self, is empty of abiding, substantial existence brings tranquillity, it can also make you passive, detached, and disengaged from life and lead to a kind of nihilistic view: "Everything is empty; nothing really matters. So why bother?"

The next step is to recognize that everything without exception has ultimate value and meaning because the rocks, the clouds, the cars, the buildings, the homeless person on the street are not separate from who you are—indeed, they're your very own essential self. Empty of substance and permanent existence, they're simultaneously filled with divinity—with radiance or presence—and therefore precious beyond price.

In Zen, this "empty fullness" finds expression in the famous words of the Heart Sutra: "Form is emptiness, emptiness is form." In other words, the world we see and hear is empty of substance, like a bubble or a dream. Yet this emptiness, this deeper ground, is never separate or apart but spontaneously expresses itself as the multidimensional play of the manifest world. If you overemphasize emptiness, you risk becoming detached, distant, and uncaring. If you overemphasize form, you risk becoming embroiled in the dream once again. Form and emptiness are inextricable, flip sides of the same coin, two faces of one seamless reality, like foreground and background, content and context, objects and space. In Zen, this nondual nature of reality is called "suchness," or "just this." In the words of a famous Zen saying, "Mountains are mountains again and rivers are rivers," but now the most ordinary experiences are glowing with spiritual significance.

Although the distinctions I'm making here may seem extremely subtle or abstract to you right now, they're actually crucial to an understanding of awakening. Until you recognize that form is not only emptiness, but emptiness is also form, you wander in what Suzanne Segal called the "wintertime" of the experience, when emptiness predominates, before the heart blossoms in the warmth and fullness of form. "When I look within and see that I am nothing, that is wisdom," says the Indian sage Nisargadatta Maharaj. But this insight must be joined by its complement. "When I look without and see that I am everything, that is love. Between these two," he concludes, "my life flows."

Some rare individuals open all at once to the complete realization that form is emptiness, and emptiness is form. For example, Robert Adams realized, in the time it took his fellow students to complete a math test, not only that he was pure awareness, the luminous void, the absolute "I am," but also that he was everything without exception: "I was the flower. I was the sky. I was the people. . . . The word 'I' encompassed the whole universe." Others may awaken first to their oneness with all things before they realize the emptiness of self, in which case they may become attached to this oneness as if it actually belonged to a me. But most of us first awaken to form is emptiness, and gradually, in fits and starts, realize the full nondual nature of reality.

UNPACKING THE ZIP FILE OF AWAKENING

Based on my own experience and my conversations with students and friends, I would suggest that most genuine spiritual awakenings contain encoded within them the full nondual realization that form is emptiness and emptiness is form—the world of kids, dogs, dishes, and work is nothing other than the lofty spiritual reality we're searching for, yet this spiritual reality doesn't exist in some distant, abstract dimension, but inevitably and spontaneously expresses itself as kids, dogs, dishes, and work.

For some reason, however, most people are unable to digest and assimilate the complete realization and instead end up with only one piece—generally, form is emptiness. They may have the felt sense that their realization contains more depth and substance than they've managed to comprehend, but they can't quite articulate or grasp it. Just as a zip file on a computer may contain many complex documents in a condensed format that can subsequently be decoded, people who awaken often download an enormous amount of insight in a single instant and then spend years unpacking and clarifying what they've received.

For example, one of my students suddenly recognized that she was the silence and stillness beneath all the noise and activity, and only gradually, in a series of further awakenings, did the silence and stillness reveal itself to be the source and substance of everything. In my own case, the luminous sphere that awakened through me felt like a hologram containing the fullness of being, but it took me years to realize this fullness and completeness, which could be most accurately expressed by the simple words "This is it!"

Even the most powerful and seemingly complete awakening may take years to unfold and reveal its riches, and further awakenings and insights are often just the deepening clarification and stabilization of what has already been received. In a sense, you could say that you may know who you are after the initial awakening, but you don't completely know what you know; you only come to realize and actualize it fully over time.

THE ENERGETIC EXPERIENCE OF AWAKENING

Distinct from the dramatic images, emotions, and sensations that may accompany spiritual awakening, the actual awakening itself is generally experienced as a subtle shift in the localization of your identity—the standpoint from which you encounter reality. My teacher Jean Klein occasionally advised his students to "find yourself behind," in the back of the head, rather than in the "thought factory" of the neocortex, located in the forehead. By this, he meant to shift your identity from the thinking mind, the self-image, the personality, to the awake, aware space behind you, the one who gazes out through every pair of eyes.

Eventually, as awakening deepens and unfolds, this more spacious localization melts into the heart center in the chest, which is where some sages consider the Self to be "located," at least on the relative, phenomenal level. Ultimately, even this most subtle localization dissolves and the Self is experienced as all-pervasive and omnipresent. In the words of the Greek philosopher Empedocles, "God [that is, true self] is a circle whose center is everywhere and whose circumference is nowhere."

DISPELLING SEVEN MYTHS ABOUT AWAKENING

Now that I've described how spiritual awakening looks and feels from the inside, I'd like to address some of the more popular misconceptions that hover around the experience like clouds. With so many books (including this one) saying so much about something that can't really be expressed in words, no wonder there's so much confusion. On the one hand, I've met folks who wander from satsang to retreat in pursuit of enlightenment, as if it were some prized archeological treasure or sacred relic they could claim as their own, bring back, and display to their friends. On the other hand, I've met people who seem content to consider themselves enlightened because they've read a few books and met a few teachers who assured them they already were. But awakening slips through your grasp when you try to achieve or possess it, and it doesn't blossom if you don't make it your own.

Myth 1: Awakening Is Just Another Spiritual Experience.

No matter how powerful they may be, most spiritual experiences turn out to be merely temporary insights or energetic states that inevitably change or fade away like images on a computer screen. After all, even the most meaningful events are impermanent by their very nature. Enlightenment is not a state or event in space and time, but the realization that you are the screen itself, the timeless, unchanging space or ground in which all states come and go, the silence behind the noise, the stillness beneath the activity.

Of course, it can be inspiring and uplifting to sense your oneness with all things, to feel a powerful outpouring of unconditional love, to undergo a dramatic surge of kundalini that lights up your chakras and sends sparks of light out the top of your head. But if these experiences aren't accompanied by a permanent shift in who you take yourself to be—by the clear knowing that you are the radiant, empty, ungraspable awareness that's looking out through these eyes right now—you still haven't awakened to your timeless, spiritual nature, and even the most exalted experiences will eventually fade into memory. Just as a sudden flash of lightning may direct your attention to the vastness of the empty sky, spiritual experiences can serve as wonderful pointers to the vastness of awareness in which they arise.

Myth 2: You Can Become Enlightened.

Similarly, enlightenment is not something you can become;
it's what you already are—yet as soon as you try to catch it
and make it your own, it eludes your outstretched fingers.
Enlightenment can never belong to a someone because
it's the clear realization that the separate someone doesn't
exist—and everything is just as it is, perfect and complete,
in the absence of a me experiencing it. Contrary to popular
opinion, spiritual awakening doesn't give you anything, it
takes away what you thought you had. In the absence of
a separate self, the incomparable and ungraspable truth of
reality reveals itself to itself.

The mind keeps trying to co-opt enlightenment and
claim it as its special prize, but its efforts are doomed to failure, like the child who keeps trying to catch the moon in a
pail. When you realize, in the words of the Upanishads, that
"I am That" (the absolute, undying Self of all), the natural
response is not pride, but profound humility, not a sense of
accomplishment, but boundless gratitude, because you see
that you're being animated and lived by the divine mystery.

Myth 3: Enlightenment Is the Pinnacle of a Process of Accomplishment and Achievement.

If you practice a progressive path, you may be told that
awakening is the end result of years of diligent effort and
devotion. Even if you don't, you may have imbibed the
popular image of the long and arduous trek up the distant
mountain of realization, which is grounded in our cultural
emphasis on success through hard work. In reality, however,

genuine awakening seems to occur more often as a sudden letting go of all effort, a spontaneous dropping of a burden you've been carrying for years, a complete and unexpected giving up of all hope—what the Twelve-Step programs call "bottoming out." You're just as likely to wake up in the midst of a crisis as in the course of a meditation retreat.

My friend and teacher Adyashanti often says that he stumbled on awakening only because he was such a failure at meditation. Eckhart Tolle went to bed one night in a paroxysm of self-loathing and woke up the next morning completely free of a sense of self. Byron Katie was living in a halfway house, consumed with rage and depression, when she looked at a cockroach walking across her foot and realized that the foot didn't belong to anyone. John Wren Lewis awakened without preparation after nearly dying of poison on a bus ride in Indonesia.

Pure wakefulness is your birthright, your natural state, and it's always present and available in every instant of awareness. You merely need to let go of all effort and die into what you already are. If crisis or suffering helps bring about this death, then so be it.

Myth 4: The Point of Enlightenment Is to Destroy the Ego.

Just as our Western preoccupation with achievement and hard work may mislead us into believing that we need to struggle toward enlightenment, we seem to have developed the misconception that awakening involves assassinating the ego and dropping its body in the ocean of the Self. But the ego isn't your archenemy, it's merely a function, a diligent worker that goes about its self-appointed task of monitoring your survival and holding on to control.

When you wake up, you see the ego for what it is—a collection of thoughts, feelings, memories, and beliefs held together by a sense of identity—and no longer mistakenly take it to be the truth of who you are or feel compelled to follow its directives. In the welcoming, nonjudgmental space that reveals itself, the ego no longer disturbs you because it has ample room to play its limited part without ruling your life. You may even feel a certain compassionate affection for its well-meaning but often misguided attempts to take care of you. Everything is perfect just the way it is, including the ego that insists it's not.

Myth 5: Awakening Involves the Improvement and Ultimate Perfection of the Me.

Many people consider the spiritual path to be the ultimate self-improvement project and expect awakening to iron out all the kinks in their personality and transform them into a kinder, holier, more virtuous version of themselves. To these folks, I say, "If you want a more perfect me, you're driving on the wrong road. Backtrack five exits and turn right at the sign marked Self-Help." The fact is, awakening frees you from your need for self-improvement because it frees you from your identification with the body, mind, and personality, which allows them to function more spontaneously and efficiently. When you no longer impose your ideas and stories about how a better, more spiritual person should look and behave, you're no longer bound by the drama of the separate self—including the story known as "self-improvement"—and can therefore be more naturally and perfectly you, with all your apparent imperfections.

Myth 6: Enlightenment Brings Omniscience and Other Extraordinary Powers.

If anything, enlightenment does the opposite—it puts you completely at ease with not knowing anything, least of all the mystery of who you really are. As I've said before, the truth of who you are can't be known by the mind, you can only be this truth knowingly. When the mind gives up trying to know, true self-realization has an opportunity to flower. The only remarkable ability that awakening confers is the freedom to act spontaneously and appropriately in each situation, without inner conflict or self-judgment. "My miraculous power and spiritual activity," admits Zen Master Layman Pang, is merely "chopping wood and carrying water."

Myth 7: You're Already Enlightened, So Why Bother Seeking?

As the flip side of the addiction to struggle and attainment, this laissez-faire approach to awakening places you outside the gateless gate I described in Chapter 1, looking in. Yes, you're already enlightened, but until this enlightenment dawns in this particular body-mind, it's just an abstract concept with little power to relieve your suffering and transform your experience of reality, which is

Breathe and Reflect

Remember that every awakening experience is unique, and yours may not resemble those you've read about in books, even this one. Ultimately, awakening is your birthright, your natural state; it's simply a matter of recognizing the awakeness that's always already present.

the whole point of the awakening process. Paradoxically, the separate self can never become enlightened, yet genuine enlightenment must take root and blossom here. Only then, in the words of an old Zen saying, can the withered tree bear fruit and the "stone woman give birth to a child in the night."

IS AWAKENING SELF-AUTHENTICATING?

How then, you may wonder, can I know whether the awakening I've had is authentic? In the Zen tradition, you're generally counseled to seek a well-established teacher who can evaluate and authenticate your awakening for you and suggest further practices to clarify and deepen it. But such teachers usually require that you join their organization and engage in regular meditation before they'll agree to meet with you individually. Besides, even if you're interested in joining, you may not happen to live in the vicinity of a Zen center. Teachers of Advaita Vedanta tend to be more accessible and plentiful, but so many claim to be enlightened and declare themselves to be teachers with only a minimum of preparation that you may find it difficult to determine which ones are qualified. For better or worse, there doesn't happen to be a licensing board for spiritual teachers!

Ultimately, only you can know for certain whether your awakening is real. Does it resemble the awakenings I described earlier in this chapter? Has the locus of your identity shifted from "small mind" to "Big Mind"—or disappeared entirely? Do you experience more contentment and peace of mind and less reactivity? Has your seeking come to an end? If you've read the teachings of the great masters and sages, you'll find that your awakening tends to authenticate itself. For most people, even those without any spiritual background, the realization is unmistakable. Eckhart Tolle didn't need a Zen master to tell him that the peace and wonder he experienced was the result of a genuine spiritual transformation. Neither did Byron Katie or Robert Adams. (In rare cases, like Suzanne Segal's, however, awakening may be temporarily mistaken for mental illness because the fear is so intense.)

In genuine awakening, the truth of your being recognizes itself through you. The process resembles looking into a mirror—you immediately identify the face as your own. The Zen tradition tells the story of a young woman who temporarily goes crazy and runs around claiming she's lost her head. Eventually, her friends and family steer her to a mirror, where she's snapped back to sanity by the sight of her own face. This parable has clear implications: The unawakened state is actually a kind of insanity that's cured in a moment of lucid self-recognition. The problems tend to arise only later, when the mind reasserts its control and begins doubting and discrediting what you've experienced or, just as problematic, claiming the realization as its own.

Ordinary, everyday awakening involves a change
of state from dreaming to waking. But spiritual
awakening seems to be different, since the
awakened person doesn't move from one reality to
another. Could you say more about that?

The metaphor of awakening can definitely be misleading. In
spiritual awakening, you wake up out of the dream of separation into the ongoing realization that there's no separate self
running the show, just this seamless, indivisible reality living
itself. The awakened person doesn't lose touch with ordinary reality the way the person who wakes up in the morning loses touch with the dream. Indeed, awakened people
seem to function more effectively in everyday life because
they act in harmony with what is, rather than in conflict or
resistance. At the same time, they see the empty, dreamlike
nature of reality—you could say that they awaken out of
the illusion of substantiality into the reality of the empty,
ungraspable nature of what is. The awakened person is "in
the world but not of it"—or as Walt Whitman put it, "in and
out of the game."

You say that the me can't wake up. What about
people who claim they're awake? Is this just
evidence of their confusion?

At the absolute level, claiming to be awake is as significant as claiming to be breathing. Awakeness is your essential nature, and you can't possibly *not* be awake. At the relative level, people who claim to be awakened may simply be using a convenient shorthand to say that the locus of their identity has shifted and they know who they really are. But those who are genuinely established in the realization of their true nature have no motivation to claim or defend any statement or position. It makes no difference to them what other people think. As my teacher Jean Klein used to say, "Our real nature can never be asserted or denied."

Wake-Up Call

Awakening to the Limitless Body of Awareness

Set aside fifteen to twenty minutes for this exploration. Begin by sitting quietly with your eyes closed for five minutes or so. Rest your awareness on the experience of sitting, and allow your body to relax. Now open your awareness to the full range of bodily sensations, which at any moment may include heat, pressure, pulsing, energy, pleasure, pain, lightness, density, and so forth. Don't focus your attention on any particular sensations, just be aware of the rich, multidimensional play of sensations throughout your body. Set aside any images or ideas you may have about your body. The only body you have is the play of sensations you're experiencing right now.

Be sure to include the sensations in your head, including the feelings of the face you take to be yours and the sensations of thoughts as they apparently arise in the brain. Set aside all names and interpretations, and experience the sensations directly, without conceptual filters.

After several minutes, allow your body's boundaries or edges to dissolve and "inner" sensations to merge with "outer" experiences. Your awareness now includes the full range of sensations both outside and inside your body. Indeed, the distinction between outside and inside no longer applies. Everything is happening inside of you.

If this doesn't make any sense yet, just keep allowing the edges to dissolve and your awareness to expand indefinitely. You feel infinite space in every direction—front, back, side to side, above and below. Who you really are is this inexhaustible awareness without center or periphery, this groundless ground that gives rise to and embraces all things. You are the limitless enjoying its expressions in form. No matter where you look, there's no separate self to be found—just this!

Keep letting go of all boundaries and concepts and surrendering to the groundless ground of inexhaustible awareness. No need to hold on to anything. This limitless vastness is what you are.

7

IN THE WAKE
OF AWAKENING

The mind is constantly trying to figure out
What page it's on in the story of itself.
Close the book. Burn the bookmark.
End of story. Now the dancing begins.

*D*uring one of the many retreats I attended with my teacher Jean Klein, I was especially impressed by the contrast between the ease and peace of mind I experienced there so effortlessly and the stressful, claustrophobic mindstate that dominated my life most of the rest of the time. Even though I had glimpsed my true nature several years before, I kept getting seduced back into believing the fears and worst-case scenarios my mind churned out in everyday life. Even though I had experienced an initial awakening, I kept falling back into a half-sleep.

When I described my situation to Jean in a group dialogue, he talked about the baggage of beliefs and psychological memory that weighed me down wherever I went, and he invited me to put it down. I was galvanized and inspired by his suggestion that I could actually drop the accumulated conditioning of a lifetime all at once, but I couldn't imagine how. The power of the mind seemed overwhelming.

After a few moments of reflection, I said, "Yes, I have a sense of what you're talking about. Deep down I know who I really am, but the old beliefs and stories are so intense that I keep forgetting."

"Ah, forgetting," he replied, with a bemused smile on his face. "The ultimate forgetting." After a period of silence, he placed his palms together and left the room. The dialogue had ended, and I was left to reflect on the power of my own forgetfulness.

FORGETTING WHO WE ARE

In the aftermath of awakening, the ultimate forgetting that Jean referred to occurs repeatedly as the mind attempts to reassert its control. Such forgetting is more than just a casual by-product of the mind's other activities: it's actually the mind's reason for being, its job description. Because the mind feels threatened by the openness, spaciousness, and mystery of spiritual awakening, it will go to great lengths to obscure it.

From an early age, we're trained by family and culture to forget the oceanic feelings of openness and oneness we're born with and to consider ourselves separate someones with particular names and identities. For example, instead of seeing a kitten, a flower, or a toy as an extension of yourself, an expression of your very own being, you learn to view it as an object out there that you can manipulate and use for your own purposes. Instead of experiencing yourself as a limitless, boundaryless field of energy and light that includes everything, both inside and outside, you're taught that you begin and end with your thoughts and your skin. Over time, this identity narrows even further as you take on more and more characteristics that both define and limit you. You're a good girl, a bad boy, a scaredy-cat, Daddy's little princess, a skilled athlete, a poor student, and so forth. Now you know who you are in the eyes of family and friends, but you've lost touch with your essential self, your true nature.

Breathe and Reflect

Have you had a glimpse of your true nature and then forgotten? How did the forgetting happen? Can you ever lose your true nature, or does it just recede into the background of your awareness? In this very instant, can you remember who you are?

Throughout childhood you experience countless interactions with parents, siblings, relatives, and friends that your mind internalizes and gradually cobbles together into a complex, multilayered representation of self and reality. Psychologist James Bugental aptly calls this the "self-and-world construct system." It's the cloudy lens or veil, made up of ideas and stories about yourself and others, through which you see yourself and the world "around" you.

When your childhood interactions are largely comfortable or pleasurable, you tend to internalize the view that you live in a benevolent world where you can relax and deal with life's circumstances as they arise. As a result, your boundaries tend to be looser and more permeable, and you find it easier to let go and allow life to unfold as it will, without tension or worry. When you experience particularly stressful or painful relationships with significant others—relationships in which you believe you risk losing their love or being intimidated, shamed, or abused if you act a certain way—you internalize the view that you need to watch out, be careful, and hold on to control at all costs. As a result, your boundaries tend to be tighter and more rigid, and you find it more difficult to relax and go with the flow of life.

Needless to say, each of us has our own unique self-and-world construct system, based on the many thousands of unique interactions and experiences we've accumulated over a lifetime, and inevitably it's a blend of positive and negative, reassuring and threatening. But whether your childhood experiences are predominantly pleasurable or painful, your boundaries primarily tight or loose, your view of life mostly benevolent or sinister, you inevitably carry with you, as an essential ingredient of your separate sense of self, the urge to control life to a greater or lesser degree.

THE TENACIOUS GRIP OF THE EGO

This need to control the flow of life because you somehow feel your well-being or survival is at stake is universal to the ordinary human condition. Generally experienced as a tension in the gut, often in the solar plexus or the lower abdomen, it's the glue that holds together the thoughts, feelings, images, and memories that make up the illusory self. As long as you believe yourself to be a separate someone, you'll continue to feel compelled to control the people and things you mistakenly perceive to be separate from and outside you. The inner mechanism or function that's programmed to maintain separation and hold on to control regardless of circumstances is often called the "ego." Essentially, the ego is an ongoing argument or struggle with the way things are. (For the remainder of this chapter, I use the terms *ego* and *self-and-world construct system* more or less interchangeably.)

In genuine spiritual awakening, you finally recognize this ego for what it is—an illusory construct held together by a sense of separateness and the need to control—and realize that you're the looker, the silent presence, the limitless space in which this construct arises. In the wake of this transformative insight, the construct loses its hold over you, at least temporarily. But because it has developed over a lifetime and gained its strength in situations where you believed your survival was at stake, the ego has tremendous power and tenacity and doesn't let go of control without a fight. In rare cases, the awakening is so complete that the separate sense of self drops away in an instant and never returns. Most of the time, however, the awakening merely shifts the location of your identity, as I described in Chapter 6; it knocks the ego from its accustomed throne as the lord of your domain but doesn't completely dismantle or disempower it. Inevitably, the ego rises again, weakened and disoriented, like an ousted dictator, and attempts to regain control of the country.

I'm playing with adversarial metaphors here because that's often the way this process is experienced by the mind. In reality, however, there's no conflict or struggle. There's only the dance of God or consciousness in manifestation, and you definitely don't need to oust the ego; you merely need to see it for what it is and rest in the spacious, all-inclusive presence that you always already are. The ego has its place in the scheme of things, its role to play—you just stop taking it to be the truth of who you are. As Ramana Maharshi says, it's merely an illusory shadow cast on the ground by the Self. I'll talk more about relating with the ego in the remaining chapters of this book.

HOW (AND WHY) THE EGO OBSCURES THE TRUTH

Although spiritual awakening itself is generally a blissful, expansive experience that may be accompanied by weeks or months of extraordinary inner peace, joy, love, and freedom from reactivity, it's often followed by an extended period of insecurity and confusion. After all, you've just experienced the most profound paradigm shift imaginable—the seeming center of your universe, the separate self you've spent a lifetime cultivating and serving, has revealed itself to be a colossal illusion. Even though you may have encountered spiritual teachings that helped prepare you for this tectonic shift in consciousness, the experience itself can be frightening and disorienting as your accustomed world collapses around you.

In particular, the ego may feel threatened by the radiant emptiness that has revealed itself to be your essence, your true nature, and it will do everything it knows how to make you forget who you are. (Remember, that's its job description, its reason for being, and it's been doing its job well for a very long time.) Committed to seeing itself as a separate someone with a particular life story—with all the suffering and exhilaration, success and failure, this story brings—the ego is terrified of being annihilated. The tactics it employs may be heavy-handed or subtle and range from trying to stuff awakening back into a conceptual box to attempting to co-opt awakening for its own purposes. But the result is the same: the clouding or distortion of the truth to which you've just awakened and the reassertion of the ego's control. Here are seven of the ego's favorite ploys.

Pretend Your Awakening Never Happened

If you had no interest in awakening in the first place or didn't realize it could be so intense and unsettling, you may try to go about your life as if nothing has changed, pretending to be interested in the same achievements, possessions, dramas, and roles as before. The problem is, the awakened view keeps reasserting itself, like an abyss opening up beneath you and revealing the emptiness at the core, or a voice speaking truth from the whirlwind beyond the mind. No matter how hard you try, you just can't get your life to fit back into the comfortable little box you once inhabited. You're in no-man's-land now, uncharted terrain. The old maps are worthless, and new maps have yet to be drawn—or more accurately, can never be drawn because reality is constantly changing and doesn't lend itself to predetermined directions. Eventually, you need to find a way to accommodate your new identity.

One of my students, for example, had a lucrative, high-profile job at a software company that gave him a sense of status and power. After his awakening, status and power lost their luster, and his work revealed itself to be inherently manipulative and dishonest. But he pushed on as if nothing had happened, attempting to talk himself out of his misgivings, because he was afraid of making changes that might cause him to lose a lifestyle to which he had become attached.

Discredit Your Awakening

Because your awakening doesn't resemble the ones you've read about in books, you may dismiss it as inauthentic. Or because you still feel angry or afraid, you may conclude that the awakening was inadequate in some way. "After all, someone like Eckhart Tolle went from self-loathing to bliss overnight," you may argue, "and his 'negative emotions' completely dropped away. Whereas I just had this moment of insight where I realized that I don't really exist. My awakening just doesn't measure up."

However, genuine awakenings come in all shapes and sizes and don't necessarily guarantee an immediate, thoroughgoing transformation in your way of being in the world. You've merely discovered who you really are—transformation follows or not, depending on how effective your ego is in its attempts to derail the process. But the spiritual superego likes to compare your insights to the enlightenment experiences of the great masters and sages and find them wanting. What better way for the ego to stay in control?

Co-Opt Awakening and Make It Your Own

Rather than allowing awakening to unfold and continue to illuminate the emptiness of self, the ego obscures the light of truth by claiming awakening as its own possession and creating the fiction of an awakened separate self, which is a contradiction in terms. The proliferation of spiritual teachers claiming to be enlightened attests to the widespread popularity of this tactic, which is known as "ego inflation," or "spiritual drunkenness." As I mentioned earlier, no one ever becomes enlightened, and awakening can't be owned in any way because it's not an object or a mind-state but the unseen subject of all objects, the mysterious and ungraspable background of all experience, the light that illuminates all phenomena. Attempt to grasp it, and it slips through your fingers. Let go of it, and it fills your hand.

Even the ultimate pronouncement "I am That" (where That refers to ultimate reality), which recurs in the Upanishads and other great spiritual texts, doesn't mean that the separate self has in any way encompassed the absolute. It simply means that the separate self is not, and only the absolute exists. In complete self-realization, any sense of identity, even with ultimate reality, dissolves in the ocean of the Self.

Yet the mind may grab hold of a particular mind-state, such as bliss or love. "How blissful or peaceful I am," the ego proudly declares to itself (and possibly to others as well). "It's a mark of my spiritual attainment." But such fabricated emotions have nothing to do with awakening and naturally

arise and pass if you allow them. Awakening is the impersonal nonstate that remains unchanged while all states come
and go.

Cycle Back and Forth Between Getting It and Losing It

"Now I have it, now I don't," thinks the mind, as it chases
the awakening it believes it once possessed but now has
somehow misplaced. Because awakening can't be owned, it
also can't be lost. But the mind mistakes a particular experience for enlightenment and keeps attempting to re-create
it. "Once I felt so open, so spacious, so loving, so empty,
and now I don't," says the mind. "Maybe this means I'm not
awakened anymore, and I'd better do everything I can to
regain it."

For this reason, the word *awakening* can be misleading;
it seems to refer to an event in space and time, whereas it's
actually the instantaneous awareness of the timeless and
boundaryless dimension of being. Even though the energetic phenomena that accompany this awareness—the rush
of bliss, the upsurge of love, the profound peace—can be
extremely appealing, the point is not to focus on the passing
states but to open to the awakeness, the timeless presence,
that's been revealed as your very own self. Just as you don't
keep trying to re-create your wedding once you're married,
but instead enjoy your partner and the life you now share,
you don't keep trying to re-create awakening, but relax and
allow awakeness to express itself through you.

Hide Out in the Transcendent

Adyashanti has observed that spiritual people tend to be more afraid of living than they are of dying, and some respond to the powerful transformational process that awakening precipitates by retreating from active participation in the world to the detached position of the disengaged witness. Also known as the "Zen sickness" or "spiritual bypassing," this tactic turns awakening from a living, breathing reality into a fixed position or point of view and prevents it from unfolding, deepening, and embodying in an ordinary, everyday way.

Claiming that there's no doer, for example, you may decline to do anything and spend your days in stubborn and determined inaction. In social situations, you may remain on the periphery, detached and undisturbed but also unresponsive and inflexible, with a smug, knowing half-smile on your face. In relationships, you may participate to the degree that suits you but pull back into a forced equanimity and insist you don't have any feelings or needs when difficulties arise. "Who, me? I never get angry or upset. After all, I don't really exist." In this way, the ego uses awakening as a pretext for remaining in control by withdrawing from a world that seems demanding, frightening, overwhelming, or chaotic. If you can't control the board, you simply refuse to play the game. (For more on spiritual bypassing, see Chapter 9.)

Fear the Emptiness

When you first awaken to the emptiness at the heart of existence, you tend to experience it as vast, radiant, silent, and infused with love. But as the fullness and richness of the experience fades, the ego may turn it into an intimidating absence of meaning and identity, a groundless abyss through which it's terrified of falling endlessly and without support. People who were inadequately nurtured and held as infants may project onto this emptiness the desolation and isolation they endured when they were young and helpless, and those who were abused may view emptiness as potentially invasive and engulfing. In essence, the ego is once again frightened of dying and losing control, even though at another level it longs for its own dissolution in the vast ocean of being. (Otherwise, why would you pursue awakening in the first place?)

My friend Suzanne Segal (whose awakening story appeared in Chapter 6) had a profound dropping away of the separate sense of self, which was followed by years of terror in the face of the absence she encountered whenever she attempted to locate herself. Finally, she met Jean Klein, who told her to simply give up this habit of trying to locate a self inside. When she followed his instructions, the emptiness of no-self gradually flowered in the fullness of the realization that everything was her very own Self.

In other words, you need to stop peering into the void from the detached perspective of the mind and instead allow the mind to dissolve into the void and peer out at the world *as* the void encountering itself. Emptiness is what you are; it's not an object of your perception. This shift inevitably releases the fear and brings deep peace and relaxation of being.

Lose Your Way in the Wintertime of the Experience

After the initial awakening to the emptiness of self, life may suddenly lose its appeal and seem dry, flat, and lifeless. "What's the point?" you may wonder. "It's all empty anyway." You may find yourself disillusioned and dissatisfied, especially if you once harbored high expectations for a life of unending bliss and delight. Suzanne Segal, who spent years in this limbo of boredom and resignation, called it the "wintertime" of the experience. Here again, the mind reifies emptiness and determines that it's empty of meaning. The only antidote is to stop conceptualizing the void and keep dying into it as a vital reality until it blossoms as the source and essence of everything. (Needless to say, the void doesn't blossom; it already is the source and essence. What blossoms is your realization.)

Breathe and Reflect

If you've had a glimpse of your true nature, consider the methods your mind has used to obscure the truth from you in order to lull you back into a half-sleep.

HOW TO RELATE TO THESE TACTICS

The most powerful approach to the mind's strategies is to recognize them for what they are—sophisticated attempts to slow down or derail the awakening process in service of the ego's need for control. They immediately loosen their grip just a little. Then ask yourself who is recognizing, and you'll find yourself free of fixation once again, resting as pure awareness itself. The more you abide as awareness—not in a dry and detached way, but energetically, with your whole being—the more these tactics will lose their hold over you, and the more your newfound identity will become deeper, more stable, and more consistent.

KINDLING THE FIRE OF TRUTH

Once you know who you are, you've ignited what Adyashanti calls the "fire of truth," which may begin as a glowing ember and end up as a raging conflagration that burns away every falsehood in its path. Truth seems to have a natural longing or determination to awaken fully to itself through us, and once you've let the genie out of the bottle, there's no use trying to stuff it back in. Your cherished beliefs, values, and assumptions are no longer safe and may be burned to ashes before your very eyes. As I noted in Chapter 2, the Tibetan teacher Chogyam Trungpa Rinpoche liked to warn his students to consider carefully before they embarked on the spiritual path, because once they had begun, there would be no turning back, and their lives would be gradually overtaken by the power of Dharma, or truth.

If you play the awakening game with the intention of gaining something for yourself, you may be startled and dismayed to discover that you're actually required to give up more than you could possibly imagine: accomplishments; comforts; identities; possessions; in short, everything you hold dear and then some. The truth demands nothing less than truth, and the journey of transformation that follows awakening involves gradually embodying and actualizing the truth you've realized in every area of your life.

I'm still not clear what happens to the so-called ego when we awaken. How can it continue when we've completely disidentified from it? Maybe it still has some important purpose or role to play.

In the nondual traditions, the term *ego* is used to refer to the glue of identification, attachment, and addiction to control that binds the various thoughts and feelings into the illusion of a separate self. When you awaken, you see through this illusion, and the glue begins to loosen its grip—though it may take a long time to let go completely. Western psychology uses *ego* somewhat differently, to refer to an essential inner function that mediates between one's instinctual drives and desires and the outside world. (In common parlance, the word *ego* is used in a variety of different ways.) When you awaken, the function of ego as Freud and his successors described it continues—you couldn't live in the world without it. At the practical, everyday level, there certainly is an inside and an outside, a mine and a yours, and the ego negotiates these distinctions quite skillfully. After awakening, however, you know that you're not the ego in any of its guises, and it no longer has control of your life.

❧

**In my years of seeking, I've lost interest in the
accomplishments and possessions that seem to
preoccupy most people, but I can't claim that I've
really awakened to who I am. I find myself saying,
"Is this all there is? There must be something more."**

You seem to be experiencing what Saint John of the Cross
called the "dark night of the soul," in which you've lost the
comfort of your familiar worldview and your accustomed
sense of self but haven't fully realized who you are. The
dark night is often likened to crossing a dry and desolate
expanse with no relief in sight, and the tendency is to fall
into depression or despair or to question the validity of the
teachings.

In my experience, this period is often intensified and
prolonged by the mind's expectations about how awakening
is supposed to look. You're constantly trying to figure reality out, rather than letting go and being present for what
is. In the simple, direct experience of what is, you have an
ongoing opportunity to awaken out of the trance the mind
perpetuates—"This isn't it. I haven't awakened yet. There
must be something more."—to the radiant fullness and completeness of being. Just keep letting go and surrendering to
what is.

❧

**But how do I let go? As you say, the ego is
programmed to hold on for dear life.**

You're right, of course. The illusory, separate self can't "do" letting go. But if you can be aware of the holding on, without resistance or judgment, the grip of ego will spontaneously loosen. Then, if you're so inclined, you can ask, "Who is aware?" (or if you've already awakened, simply remember who you are), and letting go will naturally happen.

For nondual purists who believe there's no one there to do anything, none of this makes any sense. But as long as you take yourself to be a chooser, choose to be aware and let go. When you know there's no chooser, letting go is unnecessary because it has already occurred.

Wake-Up Call

Who Do You Take Yourself to Be?

Set aside fifteen to twenty minutes for this exploration. Sit comfortably for a few minutes with your eyes closed. Now begin asking yourself the question, "Who do I take myself to be?" Make a list of all the identities, qualities, abilities, images, memories, roles, and accomplishments you take to be you. Don't hold anything back in an attempt to be spiritual. Just keep asking the question, and write down what you come up with. "I'm a great lover, a skilled conversationalist, an accomplished musician, a loving father, a devoted daughter, a renowned author, a successful attorney," and so forth. Be sure to include any spiritual identities you've accumulated over the years, such as "I'm a Buddhist, a Christian, an enlightened person, a longtime Zen student, a shaman, a psychic, a disciple of my guru, a being of light." Spend at least five minutes on this part of the exercise. (If you compile the list on your computer, print it out when you're done.)

Now pick up your list, tear it to shreds, and throw it into the wastebasket. You've wiped the slate clean, eliminated all the extras, returned to bare bones. Now ask yourself, "Who am I without these identities? What is my original face before the ego was born? Who am I really?"

If you get more conceptual answers, continue to set them aside as you inquire. The ego is endlessly adept at coming up with more identities. Just see them for what they are and ask, "Who am I really?"

8

EMBODYING THE LIGHT

When I cease to own [physical or emotional pain], I
liberate myself from its bondage and see it simply as
it is.

—Tony Parsons

*M*any seekers think of spiritual awakening as an
instantaneous transformation that emerges fully formed and
never develops or deepens. After all, didn't Prince Siddhartha
sit down under a tree and walk away eight days later as the
Buddha, the fully enlightened one? Didn't the sixteen-year-
old student Venkataraman pretend to be dead and stand up
half an hour later as the great sage Ramana Maharshi, completely merged with the Self? Even those who practice for
years to attain enlightenment expect it to occur once and for
all and ever after, like the happy ending in a fairy tale. The
traditional stories tend to support this view: the monk who
woke up when he heard a pebble strike bamboo; the master
whose body and mind "dropped away" when his teacher
hit him with a shoe; the miserable grad student who went
to sleep with a question on his lips and awakened the next
morning without the slightest vestige of a self.

Radical and complete enlightenment experiences do occur, of course, as the traditional stories attest. In these rare cases, which often make history precisely because they're so extraordinary, the light of truth drives out every last remnant of darkness and leaves the emergent sage completely transformed, with no trace of the old habits and patterns of mind that might lead to suffering and reactive, unconscious behavior.

More often, however, the initial awakening is more subtle and tentative—like a flickering candle that barely dispels the darkness rather than a bright midday sun, or a glowing coal in the fireplace rather than a raging inferno that burns down the house. Once the light is lit, you're no longer stumbling along in the dark—you see who you are once and for all, and the recognition is immediate, unmistakable, and irreversible. But, as I explained in Chapter 7, you may keep forgetting who you are, and the light of this self-recognition may not be powerful or clear enough to penetrate to every area of your life and illuminate the difficult, stuck places of work, family, relationships, or challenging emotions and habitual reactive patterns. Despite your dedication and commitment to awakening, you may find that you're still not living as the radiant mystery to which you awakened.

Many of my clients and students have described returning home from a particularly powerful retreat in which they experienced a clear recognition of their essential spiritual nature, only to immediately fly into a rage with their spouse or children or contract into a ball of fear about some insignificant concern. Needless to say, such sudden, uncontrollable outbursts can leave you wondering whether your awakening is authentic—or even questioning the value of awakening altogether.

The reality is that awakening generally occurs instantaneously, but the process of transformation that awakening initiates is often quite gradual and may take a lifetime. Once you know who you are, the question is, how can you live this understanding in every moment of your life? How can you embody the joy, freedom, love, and silent presence you know yourself to be, not just on retreat or on your meditation cushion, but in everything you do? Yet most spiritual traditions barely acknowledge this embodiment process and offer little, if any, guidance for participating in and supporting it as it unfolds.

REVEALING THE FIRE OF TRUTH

When I describe spiritual embodiment, I usually find myself drawn to the metaphors of fire and light. Just as the function of fire is to burn and the function of light is to drive out the darkness, the natural movement of truth is to illuminate and consume all the distortions, lies, self-deceptions, and self-defeating stories that have mired you in a lifetime of suffering and confusion.

When you awaken to the limitless radiance of your essential being, you uncover a fire and a light that, once revealed, have their own powerful momentum and agenda, and you may find that hiding out in your habitual patterns of reactivity, struggle, and unconsciousness becomes increasingly difficult. Wherever you're attached, fixated, or

Breathe and Reflect

Stop for a few moments and notice what you're feeling right now. Instead of affixing labels to the experience, just let it unfold in your awareness without resistance or indulgence. Drop the story and the commentary, and allow the experience to be just as it is.

addicted to control, the truth of your being, which is freedom, naturally moves to pry your fingers loose. Wherever you "numb out" or go blind, the truth, which is lucid wakefulness, whispers (or shouts) in your ear in an attempt to wake you up again. Wherever you're still deceiving yourself—living out old conditioning or failing to act in accord with the deepest truth of your being—the truth, which is radical honesty at every level, pushes and prods you to pay attention, own up, and let life live through you.

Once awakened, the fire of truth can be profoundly disturbing and unsettling as it naturally moves to embody itself through your words and actions. Let's make no mistake: Truth is a relentless power that ultimately seeks to transform your body and mind into a fluid expression of the unsurpassable peace, love, radiance, and joy that you essentially are. Sometimes this power is experienced as a ruthless energy that won't allow you to settle into familiar grooves and patterns that no longer serve your awakening. At other times, it is experienced as a warm, boundless, uncompromising compassion that naturally moves to embrace and heal all the contracted, unredeemed parts of yourself and enfold them in the light and love of your essential nature.

In the light of awakening, many people find that their old identities and their accumulated beliefs about themselves and others no longer hold any meaning and gradually drop off like ripe fruit from a tree. Like the student I described in Chapter 7, you may find that the job you took because you believed it would provide status and financial security for the fictitious little me now seems pointless, given the realization that the separate self you imagined yourself to be doesn't really exist. Or you may find that the relationship you began solely on the basis of shared personal history and future objectives now seems empty and unfulfilling, now that the objectives have lost their grip and the personal history no longer applies. Or you may find that old, unresolved emotions such as resentment or grief start bubbling to the surface to be faced and released. Many of my students complain that awakening turned their comfortable little world upside down, and no matter how hard they try, they can't go back to their old way of being.

LIVING WITH TRUE INTEGRITY

When the truth of your being is fully embodying itself from moment to moment, you're no longer struggling to maintain control of your life. Instead, you're surrendering to the current, at one with the flow, and life is living itself without effort or conflict. Rather than trying to impose your agenda on life, you're relaxed, open, spacious, awake, and attuned to the way the whole of life wants to express itself through you. You welcome what is just the way it is, because everything is experienced as inseparable from you, and you find profound contentment in the realization that this timeless moment is perfect and complete exactly as it is. This is it! In short, you're fully living the truth of the oneness and completeness to which you've awakened, rather than compartmentalizing truth and limiting it to certain parts of your life.

Ultimately, the process of embodiment demands that you live with integrity in the true sense—that is, in alignment with the deepest truth of your being. Interestingly enough, the word *integrity* itself comes from the Latin root for "oneness" or "wholeness" and refers not to following certain predetermined rules but rather to acting from the realization that life is complete and undivided. When you live in harmony and attunement with the movement of the whole, responding to situations with the knowing that everything both "inside" and "outside" you is just an expression of who you really are, you're living in integrity, whatever the rules may say. But if you act as if you're a self-interested fraction of the whole, at odds with other fractions, you're out of integrity, no matter how hard you try to follow the rules, and you inevitably cause suffering for yourself and others.

When you're out of integrity, life has a habit of sending you situations that give you an opportunity to come back into alignment with truth. For example, if you revel in the joy and peace of your true self when you walk in nature or talk with friends but find yourself withdrawing in fear when you're faced with difficult financial issues or tensing up with anger when someone threatens your power at work, truth, in its spontaneous movement to embody, will keep sending you the same kinds of challenging situations to invite you to let go of control and live by your deepest realization. Financial issues may keep disturbing you until you relax your survival fears and remember that your true nature can never be destroyed. Or coworkers may continue confronting you until you see them not as your adversaries, but as expressions of the essential self you share.

When I first studied the sixteen ethical precepts of Zen, my teacher at the time kept emphasizing that these rules of conduct, such as "don't kill, don't steal, don't lie," weren't arbitrary external standards that we should impose on our lives. Rather, he taught, they're descriptions of how a fully enlightened person naturally acts. Don't focus on following traditional guidelines. After all, circumstances are constantly changing like flowing water and can't be pinned down or defined. Instead, wake up, and the clarity of your realization will show you how to act with integrity, in accord with the precepts.

HOW THE EGO RESISTS EMBODIMENT

Essentially, my teacher was right, but he conveniently overlooked the often prolonged and challenging process of living and embodying this clarity. Whereas the truth naturally moves toward integrity, the ego—which sees you as an isolated, separate self at risk in a world of other separate selves—doesn't care about acting with integrity, though it may pretend to if that serves its purposes. Rather, it's committed to maintaining control at all costs. In fact, as I mentioned in the last chapter, control is the ego's reason for being, its job description, and it does its job well. Awakening and embodiment seem to threaten the ego's existence because they lead to letting go and moving in harmony with the flow, which is precisely what the ego is programmed to resist.

According to Western psychology, the ego emerges in early childhood as a way of mediating between inner experience and the outer environment and becomes solidified as the growing child is challenged to hold on to some semblance of security and control in uncertain, chaotic, or life-threatening situations. Even if your childhood was relatively happy and loving, you still encountered circumstances that taught you that you're separate and need to protect, defend, or promote yourself in some way. By the time you're an adult, you're attempting to exert control over some aspect of your life in virtually every waking moment.

Pay attention, and you'll notice how often you resist what is and try to get things to be different from the way they are. With friends or family, you may monitor your words and actions to make sure you elicit the love and approval you crave. In intimate relationships, you may avoid telling the truth or asking for what you want because you're afraid of causing conflict. Behind the wheel of your car, you may honk, speed, and complain about the traffic and the other drivers as you rush to work. Moving through your day, you may control the environment constantly to maintain the most comfortable state of body and mind. Spiritual egos aren't immune to this addiction to control. Indeed, they may be the most flagrant addicts of all, as spiritual people seem committed to achieving and sustaining experiences of love, tranquillity, and bliss and avoiding "negative" emotions like anger or fear.

Fortunately, the ego gradually loosens its grip as the journey of awakening unfolds. In the light of the initial awakening, which reveals the emptiness of the separate self, some of the more blatant forms of manipulation and control simply become untenable. For example, you may stop "power-tripping" your employees or yelling at your kids because the boundaries between self and other have suddenly dissolved and you can no longer treat others as if they were separate from you. Then, as awakening deepens and spreads and you live more and more consistently from the awakened per-spective, the ego may relax its hold even further as it realizes that life continues just as effectively—even turns out to be infinitely more satisfying and harmonious—when you let go and let life live through you.

Most of the time, however, the ego will stubbornly con-tinue to maintain control over certain areas of your life, even after you've awakened. "I can relax and let go in relationships or with family and friends," your ego may concede, "but I have to hold on tight when it comes to money or health." One of my students, for example, had a series of profound realizations that transformed his life in countless ways, but he continued to obsess over his health and couldn't trust consciousness or true self to take charge of this area of his life as well. Trust is the core issue here: Egos are programmed to distrust because they develop in early life in response to uncertain or untrustworthy situations. If you've had a happy childhood and your lack of trust is minimal, your ego tends to let go readily. But if you've experienced repeated betrayals of trust in the form of disappointment, abandonment, or abuse, your ego may hold on for dear life because it doesn't trust the ground of being to support you. Beneath the ego's tenacious demand for control generally lie core stories or beliefs about life that need to be acknowledged and investigated.

Lest I give the ego a bad rap, I want to emphasize that it's not your enemy, it's a dedicated general in what it perceives to be the battle called life. It may have guided and protected you through difficult times, and it believes it must be constantly vigilant. The problem is that once you awaken, you realize that the belief that life is a battle is merely a construct created by the mind and perpetuated by the ego. You could say that the ego is the screenwriter, director, producer, and star in the movie called *Life*, but none of it has anything to do with you. When you step out of the film into the clear light of reality, the ego no longer has a role to play and may let go of control completely. Or more often, it may retreat to some stronghold deep inside where it maintains control at a subtler, more unconscious level. Either way, the love that you are ultimately embraces the ego as a devoted servant that has mistakenly assumed the role of master. In reality, it's just a function or mechanism without any substantial or abiding reality.

HOW TO SUPPORT THE EMBODIMENT PROCESS

At this point, you may be wondering what you can do to help facilitate the process of embodiment. Let me begin by reminding you that the "you" that believes it can do something to make embodiment happen is merely the ego in disguise, attempting once again to impose its agenda on life. "There's something wrong here, something missing," the ego inevitably believes. "I'm not fully embodied enough, whatever that might mean, and I need to remedy the situation as soon as possible." But full and complete embodiment is available right here and now when you let go, stop resisting and controlling life (including the so-called embodiment process), and allow everything to be just the way it is.

"Then how can I let go and stop resisting?" you may wonder. Here again, you might ask whether the ego is merely seeking another strategy for becoming a better, more spiritual you. You can't "do" letting go—it just happens naturally as the light of awakening illuminates the innumerable places where you're still holding on. If there's any strategy, it's this: Stay awake! When you feel the grip of the ego in your belly, the contraction in your heart, the tensing of your shoulders as you once again hold on and resist what is, stop and inquire, "Who is aware of this right now? Who am I really?" In an instant, you may find yourself out of the process, once again expanded, spacious, awake, and nonreactive. Now abide knowingly as this spacious awareness without trying to change the external situation in any way.

In general, the path of embodiment asks that you live your understanding from moment to moment. As my friend and teacher Adyashanti put it, serve the truth you know yourself to be. Rather than allowing yourself to fall back into old patterns, live the silent presence—the empty fullness, the openness, peace, and clarity you experienced when you woke up—in every situation. In other words, be who you are.

This requires what my teacher Jean Klein called earnestness or sincerity, a deep, abiding commitment to the truth in all circumstances. Awakening tends to ignite it, but this commitment may flag from time to time as the ego puts up a fuss. If you appear to have a choice, choose the truth again and again—not only the absolute truth of your being but the relative truth of the moment. In its efforts to maintain control, the ego tends to fudge, obscure, or avoid the truth in order to manipulate situations for its own benefit. Instead, the process of embodiment asks that you tell the truth and let go of the outcome, which involves a major leap into the unknown.

For example, you may be accustomed to telling white lies in your relationship to avoid conflict and elicit your partner's approval, but you compromise your commitment to truth in the process. What would your relationship be like if you kept telling the truth of your experience, not in a brutal or judgmental way, but gently and honestly? What if, instead of trying to manipulate your partner into giving you what you want, you just asked for it and allowed your partner the freedom to say no if he or she felt inclined? Are you ready to let go even that much, be that vulnerable, and welcome the unknown? If you're not, you end up sacrificing your own awakeness and lulling yourself back to sleep again.

LIVING WITHOUT A STORY

When you're fully embodying the truth of your being, you're living not as the story you've taken yourself to be for a lifetime, but as the pure, empty, radiant wakefulness you've always essentially been. Instead of imagining yourself to be the personal center around which the drama of your life story plays itself out, you're now the vast, unencumbered space in which life itself unfolds as an

Breathe and Reflect

Begin by sitting quietly with your eyes closed. Now open your eyes and look around while telling yourself the story that you're trapped in this terrible, unworkable life circumstance, and nothing is the way you want it to be. Notice how you feel. Close your eyes, and when you open them again, look around while telling yourself the story that everything is perfect just the way it is—indeed, it's God or spirit in manifestation. Notice how you feel now.

impersonal mystery, with your body-mind as just one part of the total manifestation. Now you're free to respond not from psychological memory, but from the limitless freshness, openness, and compassion of don't-know mind. Many people experience this way of being for extended periods of time after they awaken but then seem to lose it as awakening fades into the background and old stories reassert themselves.

While living in a halfway house after years of depression and rage, Byron Katie woke up to her essential nature when she saw a cockroach walk across her foot and realized that the foot didn't belong to a someone. The sense of a separate self had completely dropped away, and she was reborn as innocent wakefulness, without a life history or even a name. Yet every time Katie found herself "velcroing" to a thought, as she put it, she noticed that she began to suffer again. So she developed a process of inquiry that allowed her to investigate and release the thoughts and stories that caused her pain. Out of this firsthand experience, the Work of Byron Katie emerged. Katie initially called it the "Great Undoing," because it allowed her to release the grip of the stories that kept returning to haunt her—until they didn't any longer.

Just as you can use self-inquiry to turn your attention back on the Self and invite an initial awakening to the truth of your being (see Chapter 5), you can use the Work and other forms of investigation to question the beliefs and stories that flood back to fill the space that awakening reveals. "I'm not good enough. I'm not safe. Life is a struggle. Nobody loves me," you may find yourself believing again. In response, you can ask the questions that Katie and others recommend: "Is it really true? Can I really know that it's true? How do I respond when I believe this thought? Who would I be without it?" With dedicated self-inquiry, the stories gradually lose their hold and recede into the background or dissipate altogether, and you once again rest as open, unfurnished awareness or presence, without center or periphery. This natural movement of resting and inquiring is like the alternation of the left and right foot in walking.

As long as you appear to have a choice, choose to rest or abide as much as possible as the open, unfurnished awareness and limitless love of your essential nature, and meet each story or belief with inquiry. Eventually, resting and inquiring become choiceless and effortless, like the blinking of your eyes or the beating of your heart, and embodiment naturally deepens and expands. Particularly tenacious or deeply rooted "core stories" (known as *samskaras* in the Advaita tradition and *kleshas* in Buddhism) may invite more focused investigation, as discussed in Chapter 9.

EMBODIMENT THROUGH THE CHAKRAS

As its name implies, the embodiment of awakening tends to move down through the chakras (the seven energy centers) from the upper realms of spiritual illumination through the heart and into the body and the more instinctual centers. For many people, the initial awakening takes the form of a profound insight into the empty nature of reality and the nonexistence of the separate self. But this insight may remain just a powerful spiritual idea or, at best, a shift in perspective unless it's fully received by the heart and allowed to transform the way you relate to life.

For example, the realization that you're pure, limitless wakefulness or presence is centered in the upper chakras and may afford you tremendous equanimity and detachment. But until this realization descends and blossoms into the deeper knowing that everyone and everything you meet is the same presence, the same true self or Buddha nature, you haven't awakened your heart and allowed the boundless love and compassion of your essential self to flow. With the awakening of the heart, the dry, detached perspective of the disengaged witness, which still involved a subtle separation between self and other, dissolves into the unconditional love that includes and embraces everything without exception. The awakened heart is not limited to the energetic center in the chest, but ultimately reveals itself to be the limitless ground of reality, the current of love that animates all things. As Nisargadatta Maharaj puts it, "When I look within and see that I'm nothing, that's wisdom. When I look without and see that I'm everything, that's love."

As powerful as it may be, abiding as the heart is just the beginning of an even deeper phase of embodiment. If you have unresolved issues, core stories, or karmic knots in the lower chakras, you may still have difficulty expressing the love and wisdom that you are in a practical, embodied way when you feel challenged or threatened. For example, if you were often shamed or overpowered as a child, you may forget who you are and lash out in anger when you feel criticized or judged and may even be inclined to impose your ideas and judgments on others. If you were often abandoned or rejected, you may react with terror or rage when you sense significant family members or friends withdrawing their approval or love. And if you didn't feel safe or supported, you may constantly feel insecure or distrustful about your physical or financial survival.

Because these lower-chakra concerns are so deeply imprinted, they tend to overshadow or sabotage the more recent and tentative realization of your essential nature. No matter how awakened your heart and mind may be, you keep getting ambushed by strong emotional reactions that grip your body and don't readily respond to the spiritual knowing of your upper chakras. In his bestselling book *Emotional Intelligence*, Daniel Goleman calls this "emotional hijacking."

As the embodiment of truth continues, the love that you essentially are naturally moves down into the lower chakras to embrace and redeem these core stuck places just as light, by its very nature, seeks to illuminate every last vestige of darkness. In the process, old habits and difficult emotions may get activated, and you may end up feeling as though awakening has caused you more suffering than it's relieved. At this point, you may be moved to work more closely with these deeply ingrained reactive patterns, as I'll discuss in the next chapter.

You talk about the importance of telling the truth. But sometimes telling the truth seems to get me into trouble.

It depends on what you mean by truth. In my work as a therapist, I encourage my clients to tell the "unarguable truth"—that is, the truth of their experience that can't be refuted or contested. This truth describes your own feelings and sensations; it doesn't make controversial claims about other people or situations. For example, statements like "You're being abusive" or "You say you love me, but you really don't" aren't the truth; they're merely your opinion and will no doubt prompt a strong reaction in others. If you say instead, "When you talk to me like that, I feel tense and angry," or "When you forget to call me when you say you will, I feel a pain in my heart and find myself doubting your love for me," you're telling the unarguable truth. No one can really argue with these statements, though they may not appreciate the implications. Instead of attacking or defending, you're being open and vulnerable and available for a genuine, truthful response.

The embodiment process you describe sounds suspiciously like the progressive approach of practicing to make myself a better, more effective vehicle for truth. What's the difference?

First of all, you can't do embodiment as you would a practice. Embodiment begins to happen spontaneously as the truth to which you've awakened naturally moves to express itself in every area of your life. Once you've seen the truth of your being, you just can't live the same lies anymore, and as you get clearer, the lies become more blatant.

Besides, truth has its own intelligence and moves to free you in mysterious ways, whereas cookie-cutter practices pretend to know what truth will require of you but actually can't, because they're prepackaged and don't take into account the uniqueness of your being and life situation.

In any case, progressive practices tend to distract your attention from truth and make you a great seeker but an unfulfilled finder. Wake up now, and let the truth embody itself as it will.

But if I practice some of the progressive techniques before I awaken, won't the postawakening process go more smoothly?

Maybe—or maybe not. As I've mentioned before, progressive techniques reinforce the belief in a separate self who's causing awakening to happen, which just makes the belief more difficult to drop. Sometimes people who have practiced meditation for years before awakening have an easier time recognizing and embracing the shift in identity that awakening brings. But such seasoned meditators may also hold on stubbornly to their spiritual beliefs and have a more difficult time letting go and letting truth take its course.

In the case you describe, the mind is preoccupied not with awakening, but with making "the postawakening process go more smoothly," whatever that might mean. How can you possibly know how the postawakening process should go? Why not leave that to God, who's in charge of it anyway, and focus your attention on discovering who you are instead?

Wake-Up Call

Mirror, Mirror, on the Wall

Set aside ten to fifteen minutes for this exploration. Begin by sitting quietly with your eyes closed in front of a large mirror. Relax and breathe. After a few minutes, open your eyes and gaze into your reflection. Don't concentrate or focus in any way. Let your gaze be soft and loving. If you find yourself looking away, gently return to your reflection.

At first you may notice a litany of judgments and comments: "I look old, tired, unattractive. See the bags under my eyes or the sagging beneath my chin. I need a haircut, a shave, a perm, a face-lift. No wonder no one wants to date me." The possibilities are endless. Indeed, most of us rarely look at ourselves in the mirror without an accompanying story. Notice the commentary, let it go, and continue your soft and affectionate gaze.

Many people report that their parents failed to really see and accept them as they were when they were children. Here you have an opportunity to provide this acceptance for yourself.

As the layers of judgment drop away, you may notice waves of emotions arising—grief for past pain, fear for the future, anger about unresolved injustices. Let these feelings pass through without attaching to them or trying to understand them, and continue to gaze.

Eventually, you may find yourself connecting with the essence behind the appearance, the true self beneath the stories and feelings, the inner light that radiates out through your eyes. You may experience the form in front of you dissolving into empty space. Or you may realize that the one who is looking is not the person you see in the mirror. Whatever happens, take note of it as you continue your soft and affectionate gazing. When you're done, notice how your experience of yourself has changed.

9

FREEING THE DARK
INSIDE THE LIGHT

This bright Self wants to liberate all of itself and truly
love itself in all of its flavors. This brightness comes
back for itself, for every bit of confusion, for every bit
of its suffering.

—*Adyashanti*

My first Zen teacher, a gentle eccentric, preferred
spontaneous improvisation to traditional ritual and encouraged his students to practice what he called "guerrilla Zen,"
that is, meditating on your own, in the midst of career and
family and the other demands of everyday life. I loved him
like a father, but over the years, I became impatient with his
unconventional approach. After all, I'd ordained as a monk,
and I was eager to engage in some of the intensive, no-
holds-barred Zen training I'd read about in books. I wanted
to devote myself to the monastic life, not live out my days
meditating in someone's converted garage in the suburbs of
San Francisco.

Eventually, I went off to study with another teacher
who boasted impressive credentials (he was recognized as
enlightened in three different lineages) and seemed committed to a more traditional approach to Zen practice.
Shortly after moving to the center he headed, however, I
was surprised to discover that he didn't live up to my image
of how an enlightened person should act. Unlike my first
teacher, who was the embodiment of kindness and patience,
the roshi was prone to angry outbursts when things didn't
go his way. During breaks in the regular schedule, he would
get predictably and often quite publicly intoxicated, and
when I became his personal attendant, I discovered that he
would give one-on-one interviews with his students while
still under the influence. Later I learned that several women
left the center after he made sexual advances toward them
during interviews. Under the pretense of enlightened behavior, I found, the roshi was acting in unskillful and self-serving
ways that caused harm to others.

Because I was hungry for the Dharma and the promise
of spiritual "advancement" he offered, I managed to avoid
confronting my concerns and remained for nearly five years
before putting aside my robes and leaving to study Western
psychology. In the end, I came to the conclusion that if
this teacher was the role model for what Zen had to offer,
traditional practice alone wasn't going to make me a saner,
wiser, more compassionate, and less reactive human being; I
felt I needed to learn more about the workings of the human
mind and heart before I taught others. Two years after I left,
the center disintegrated when the roshi was caught lying

about an affair with one of his senior students and alcohol rehab didn't seem to change his fundamental disposition. I'd experienced my first lesson in the potential consequences of spiritual bypassing.

THE EFFECTS OF SPIRITUAL BYPASSING

Spiritual bypassing is the tendency to hang out in the spacious emptiness of the upper chakras (see Chapter 8) and use the nondual language of spiritual realization as an excuse to avoid or ignore the troublesome behavior patterns or challenging psychological or emotional issues that prevent us from living this realization from moment to moment. In essence, spiritual bypassing is yet another, more sophisticated way for the ego to maintain its control over our lives.

For example, people who bypass may act thoughtlessly or insensitively but refuse to examine or take responsibility for their actions, because they claim awakening has freed them from the constraints of conventional behavior (an argument frequently advanced in defense of the roshi). Or they may be prone to intense emotional outbursts that they dismiss as merely passing phenomena with no abiding significance—despite the impact these outbursts have on the people around them. Or they may remain on the periphery of life because they're afraid of engaging, claiming it's all just a dream, so there's no point in getting involved.

Meditation centers and ashrams are filled with spiritual bypassers who sit blissfully on their cushions in a kind of manufactured *samadhi* (one-pointed attention) or move fluidly and radiantly through their yoga routines, then go

Breathe and Reflect

Stop and consider your own favorite brand of spiritual bypassing. How do you use your spirituality to avoid the complexities of your human embodiment? How do you forsake your vulnerability for spiritual defensiveness, your tenderness for detachment, or your natural engagement for an artificial transcendence?

home and yell at their kids, get regularly stressed out about money or work, or have difficulty functioning in everyday life. Does any of this sound familiar? Needless to say, the roshi was just a more visible example of tendencies to which all of us are prone.

By its very nature, of course, spiritual awakening inevitably involves a certain measure of spiritual bypassing. When you awaken to your essential, undivided, spiritual nature, you leapfrog over your conditioning and realize yourself as the silent presence that is untouched and undisturbed by any thoughts or emotions, no matter how challenging they once may have seemed. Now your conditioning arises and passes away in the vastness of who you are and no longer appears problematic. Now only the timeless dimension exists, and the time-bound, phenomenal realm is experienced as merely the play of the Divine. Because awakening generally eliminates at least a certain amount of conditioning and leaves you freer and less reactive, you may believe that your journey is complete. But the lifelong process of deeper embodiment has usually just begun.

At this point, you may be tempted to turn awakening into a fixed position or point of view, a new identity to which you become attached, another filter through which you relate to life. "After all, I've spent years in search of awakening," you may think, "and I've finally attained it. Awakening belongs to me, it defines who I am. I'm an awakened person now, and I'm free to do what I wish." Traditionally, this fixation on awakening as an identity is known as Zen sickness, and it's notoriously difficult to cure, since it's so seductive and self-fulfilling. In Zen sickness, the ego once again co-opts awakening and turns it into its own little fiefdom. By contrast, genuine awakening is the complete absence of any fixation or identity and can't be turned into a position or point of view.

Spiritual bypassing is an inevitable phase and only becomes problematic when the awakened position (an oxymoron if ever there was one) becomes entrenched. Teachers are particularly susceptible to spiritual bypassing because they've established themselves as the purveyors of spiritual wisdom, and their power and status depend on maintaining and defending their authority. Several years after I left the roshi to study Western psychology, I happened to meet him at a conference, and he invited me for tea. After some initial pleasantries, our talk turned to the breakup of the center, and he became visibly angry and defensive. When I gently suggested that he might still harbor some feelings about what had occurred there, he heatedly countered that it no longer bothered him in the least.

Most nondual spiritual traditions inadvertently encourage spiritual bypassing by providing little or no guidance for embodying the profound shifts and insights that accompany awakening. These traditions are primarily concerned with revealing the eternal and tend to let the mundane concerns of everyday life take care of themselves. For example, the teachings of Advaita Vedanta, which emphasize that there's no separate doer and that every occurrence is merely the play of the Divine, offer welcome relief for those who have spent their lives on an endless treadmill of efforting and self-improvement. Finally, you awaken to the realization that everything is perfect just the way it is, nothing is lacking or out of order, and the you who keeps practicing to make yourself better is merely an illusion. But Advaita's focus on inherent perfection can leave the mistaken impression that spiritual transformation is complete once an initial awakening has occurred, and everything you do thereafter, no matter how unskillful or self-serving, is a perfect expression of the Divine. One contemporary Advaita teacher, obviously laboring under this misconception, made sexual advances to his students, then refused to take responsibility, claiming that the body-mind mechanism was merely acting according to its conditioning and he had nothing to do with it.

In Zen, koan study is often touted as a method for practicing the actualization and embodied expression of your innate Buddha nature. In reality, however, koan study tends to be a ritualized give-and-take that occurs in private, in a sequestered environment, and doesn't necessarily generalize to the world of money, power, and personal relationships. Besides, most koans describe cryptic exchanges that took place between monks and their teachers in an unfamiliar culture hundreds of years ago, and their relevance to the blood and guts of everyday life may seem tentative at best. The roshi I spoke of earlier had completed koan study in two separate traditions, and I've watched over the years as a succession of his students have acted in the most outrageous and insensitive ways, despite years of koan work.

Clearly there are cultural reasons for this traditional lack of attention to spiritual embodiment. In the East, most serious seekers spent their lives in monasteries or ashrams, where their behavior was carefully circumscribed by institutional precepts and guidelines that described exactly how to behave. Traditional societies also had well-defined ethical rules and role expectations that left no doubt, for example, how men and women should relate to one another or how members of different classes or hierarchical levels should interact. In the case of the roshi, it wasn't considered culturally appropriate for the other Zen masters in his lineage to monitor the inconsistencies between his behavior and his purported realization, and his students were too intimidated by his spiritual stature and pedigree (and his rather fierce demeanor) to confront him on his spiritual bypassing. Even his wife, who was originally one of his students, seemed as cowed in his presence as everyone else.

In the contemporary West, by contrast, we live in a much more fluid and nonhierarchical social environment in which authenticity, spontaneity, and direct communication are valued over socially correct or conformist behavior. As a result, we're called on to respond to situations intuitively as they unfold, and our responses and the frank responses of others provide ongoing feedback about whether we're living the awakened reality of no-self and no-separation or living from attachment to our fixed point of view. In addition, our personal relationships are far more complex and psychologically sophisticated, and our friends, partners, and family members require that we bring a fullness of being and an authenticity of emotional expression to our interactions that weren't expected in the traditional East.

Let me be clear, however: Embodiment is not about becoming a better person or living up to the expectations of yourself or others; the mind is just thrilled at the prospect of turning embodiment into another self-improvement project. Rather, it's about freedom and authenticity, about letting the radiant emptiness that you are live your life, not the conditioned mind with its preconceived ideas and agendas. When you're embodying the truth, you're living without conflict or resistance, in harmony with the flow of what is.

COMMITMENT TO DEEPER EMBODIMENT

Despite our cultural emphasis on authenticity, there are still plenty of opportunities for avoiding the embodiment process, even in the West. For example, ashrams, meditation centers, and other spiritual communities and groups often mimic the culture on which they're based by encouraging the use of spiritual jargon and conformity to traditional guidelines, rather than authentic action and self-expression. Ultimately, East or West, only a deep and wholehearted commitment to the truth at every level can undermine the natural tendency toward spiritual bypassing and keep dismantling the various fixations the ego tends to construct.

The fire of truth must burn bright enough that you desire complete freedom more than the power, comfort, or recognition that the "awakened position" can confer. As a result, you're willing to face the reactive patterns, the contracted knots of suffering and control; acknowledge that the truth has not yet fully embodied itself in your life; and be open to allowing the love and awareness of your essential nature to enter.

This unflinching investigation requires a discriminating wisdom that sees reality as complete and perfect just the way it is, yet at the same time acknowledges the relative imperfections, the stuck places that awakening has yet to illuminate and redeem. Through the eyes of such wisdom, you recognize the seamless, undivided nature of reality yet can discriminate between absolute and relative truths (see Chapter 1): "Yes, I realize that I'm nothing but pure consciousness, but somehow I still suffer, still get embroiled in the drama of life and contract in fear or explode in anger, still act unskillfully and cause harm to others." "I know that I'm Buddha nature incarnate, but I don't live every moment with the peace, love, and freedom of the fully enlightened one." As Zen Master Shunryu Suzuki said, "We're constantly losing our balance in a world of perfect balance." There's no judgment or blame in this recognition, just the steadfast, unwavering gaze of truth, because you realize that the imperfections and imbalances are inevitable and have nothing to do with who you really are. Here again, we encounter the core paradox: everything is perfect just as it is—but when the roof leaks, have it repaired.

As I suggested earlier, those who suffer from Zen sickness tend to get caught in the absolute perspective and turn it into a fixed position. As a result, they can act insensitively and unskillfully because they refuse to recognize that ego still controls their behavior in unrecognized ways—that is, they haven't fully embodied. My friend and teacher Adyashanti had a series of deepening awakenings over a period of years, and after each one (except the last), he heard a voice that told him, "This isn't it, just keep going." That's the kind of relentless commitment to truth that fuels the process of spiritual embodiment.

FREEING THE EMOTIONAL BODY

Genuine spiritual awakening shatters the comfortable little world of personal beliefs and identities you've constructed over a lifetime and reveals your true nature as the vastness of being. Though the old stories tend to come back and reassert their control, they generally dissolve rather quickly in the light of investigation and inquiry. Once your mind has been swept clean of concepts, at least temporarily, it's easier to identify and release the concepts as they arise. Once you have a direct insight into the emptiness of self, it's hard to pretend to be someone for long.

But emotional identification tends to be more deeply rooted and "endarkened," and it doesn't respond as readily to the light of awakened awareness. You may know who you are and be relatively free of fixed beliefs and stories—or at least recognize them as they arise without getting attached—yet keep reacting to circumstances in a powerful, visceral way that belies your spiritual understanding. Awakening has illuminated your upper chakras but has not yet reached down into your emotional centers, where ego has established a more inaccessible stronghold. Most of the people I know who have had powerful awakening experiences still get ambushed by their emotions at least occasionally, if not regularly, and many are aware of an ongoing contraction in one or more of the emotional centers that signals an unawakened fixation of emotional energy, a stuck place that has the potential at any moment to flare up into reactivity and suffering.

Many Eastern spiritual traditions ignore the emotional dimension entirely and prefer to encourage transcendence and bypassing. The renowned Japanese Zen master Eihei Dogen once characterized zazen (Zen meditation) as "dancing on the heads of demons," by which he meant that the power of concentration generated in meditation creates a kind of force field of purity and wakefulness that keeps the so-called negative emotions and defilements at bay. When I studied Zen in the 1970s, we were encouraged to develop the power of samadhi and intensify our focus when our emotions proved difficult or problematic. (More recently, Zen has been influenced by Western psychotherapy and become somewhat more sensitive to emotional issues.) The Indian tradition of Advaita Vedanta invites the seeker to release the hold of the negative emotions by seeing their inherently insubstantial, illusory nature and realizing that the separate self to which they apparently belong simply doesn't exist.

These strategies may be effective at maintaining wakefulness in the midst of challenging circumstances, but they often fail to transform the more difficult, persistent emotional patterns and instead merely drive them deeper beneath the surface, where they're no longer visible but still exert a powerful influence. For example, one well-known American Zen teacher who was renowned for his clarity had a series of covert affairs with his students but refused to apologize or acknowledge the inappropriateness of his behavior when he was finally confronted. Another, whose samadhi could light up a room, created quite a stir in the neighborhood when he chased a stranger down the street with a gun. In traditional cultures, such behavior by teachers might have been excused or ignored. But in the contemporary West, where honesty and accountability are prized, emotional embodiment is necessary, lest we wreak havoc in our communities and personal relationships and heap suffering on ourselves.

Perhaps the primary problem with these strategies for dealing with the emotions is that they are, indeed, "strategies," effortful tactics designed to avoid or eliminate the emotions rather than welcome them as a natural expression of the human condition—and as another perfect manifestation of your essential nature. This strategic approach reflects an aversive, adversarial attitude toward the emotions that permeates not only Eastern religions but traditional religions throughout the world. If you aspire to be a spiritual person, these traditions teach, you need to cultivate the so-called positive qualities and mind-states and eliminate the negative—an approach that's inherently dualistic and encourages an inner division or conflict that's impossible to assuage. As long as you deem some experiences desirable and others undesirable, you're destined to be at war with yourself—and war is ego's favorite activity. As long as you're attempting to get rid of some aspect of yourself, even in the subtlest way, you merely afford the ego more power.

From the nondual perspective, the key to working with disturbing emotions and core reactive patterns is to meet them with genuine love and acceptance—what Nisargadatta Maharaj called "affectionate awareness"—without indulging in the drama they convey and without subtly, or not so subtly, pushing them away. Consciousness or awareness, your essential nature, spontaneously meets and delights in each arising, without preference or resistance. In the vastness and completeness of who you are, nothing is experienced as unacceptable or left out.

If there's any technique here, it's to abide as awareness and welcome your emotions as you would your most intimate friends. Give them plenty of space to express themselves, but don't energize or solidify them by resisting them or taking them to mean something about a fictitious me. Not *my* sadness, but *the* sadness; not *my* anger, but *the* anger. Eventually, even these minimal labels drop away, and you're left with the raw, sensate experience of the moment, free of any story. The emotions may dissipate and release (they generally do), or they may stick around—you're not attached to the outcome. When you rest as the silent, empty mystery of your essential nature, which is the undisturbed yet welcoming background of every experience, this kind of intimacy occurs quite naturally, without any direction or effort, as the spontaneous movement of love and compassion.

In his poem "The Guest House," the Persian mystic Rumi accurately likens this intimacy to being a gracious and open-hearted host to the full range of human experience. "Welcome and entertain them all," he says of uninvited guests like depression or meanness. "The dark thought, the shame, the malice, meet them at the door laughing and invite them in." Rather than considering them unwelcome intruders, he encourages us to feel grateful for these difficult emotions, as they provide an opportunity to open more fully. The more we try to exclude these guests and fortify our realization as if it were some unassailable citadel, as certain traditions teach, the more rigid and narrow we become and the more genuine realization slips through our fingers. By contrast, the more wholeheartedly we accept and embrace whatever arises, the more we abide as the spaciousness and expansiveness of consciousness itself, our essential nature, which includes everything without exception.

Here's an example of how the process of emotional embodiment may unfold. Let's say you've been feeling grief and sadness for weeks about the loss of a significant relationship, and the emotions haven't spontaneously released but have become fixated and repetitive. Talking or writing about them doesn't seem to help, and even allowing them to be, without consciously indulging or avoiding them, hasn't shifted your suffering. Clearly, you're caught in identification and attachment.

If you can genuinely recognize—not as an intellectual concept but as a whole-body realization—that there's no separate little me to which these feelings apply and that your life is actually unfolding in some perfect, impersonal, and mysterious way, the feelings will gradually (or suddenly) dissipate and release. As Byron Katie likes to say, they've come to pass and not to stay.

If they continue to haunt you, you can inquire into the beliefs that perpetuate them; for example, "I'll never meet someone like that again," "It was my fault," or "I'm all alone in the world." For each story, you can ask, "Is it really true?" "How do I react when I believe this story?" and "Who would I be without it?" In response to such concerted inquiry, persistent beliefs and the feelings they cause tend to loosen their hold. Again, you're not trying to get rid of them, you're just freeing yourself from the suffering that results when you attach to them.

ENLIGHTENING THE ENDARKENED

Some emotional patterns and recurring identities and stories seem to be more deeply entrenched than others and don't readily shift or loosen their grip in the embrace of affectionate awareness or the investigation of self-inquiry. You could say that they constitute the underlying root, hidden beneath the surface, from which passing emotions such as anger and fear keep springing up, like shoots and branches.

In Hinduism and Buddhism, these persistent root patterns (called *samskaras*, Sanskrit for "impressions") consist of the imprints left on the mind by experiences (in both this life and past lives) that color future experiences, behaviors, and states of mind. From the perspective of Western psychology, which has paid particular attention to their evolution, these root patterns (called object relations, or complexes) develop over the lifespan as the result of repeated experiences that reinforce the same distorted point of view. Considered the focus of long-term depth psychotherapy, they're so tenacious precisely because ongoing life experiences provide convincing evidence for their validity. These patterns range from a tendency to fixate and obsess about certain life issues, especially those that appear to be survival-related, to entire subpersonalities and split-off parts of the psyche that have their own autonomy, like separate selves.

After moving into a cave high in the Himalayas and setting up his meditation cushion, the renowned Tibetan yogi Milarepa discovered that the cave was inhabited by a company of noisy, mischievous demons. At first, he tried to subdue them, but they just became more boisterous. (Unlike Dogen, apparently, he didn't have the option of dancing on their heads.) Realizing that his approach was both violent and futile, he decided to send the demons love and compassion instead—at which point, half of them departed. Loosening his grip even further, he surrendered to hosting the remaining demons indefinitely, instead of trying to get rid of them, and he invited them to stay as long as they liked. All but one particularly mean and ferocious demon left. Finally, Milarepa gave up every attempt to control his situation, and with utmost love and compassion, he placed his head in the demon's mouth as an offering. The demon vanished and never returned.

Like Milarepa, most of us tend to struggle with challenging emotional patterns at first, trying to change, improve, or eliminate them through a variety of self-help techniques. Next we may turn to meditation in a concerted attempt to generate enough peace of mind, insight, and compassion to drive the patterns away through the power of our spiritual practice. Once we awaken, we may keep applying the spacious, open, unconditioned awareness of our essential nature to these patterns in the hope that they'll dissipate in the light of our wakefulness. Many of the patterns do release in response to these tactics, but the most resistant and ferocious ones require our complete surrender and acceptance before they let go of their hold over us.

Repression and Dissociation

In the months and years that follow awakening, many people experience a flood of difficult or upsetting emotions, including some they never knew existed. They may feel rage or terror or other feelings with an unfamiliar intensity, or find themselves overwhelmed with sadness or grief for long-ago losses they thought they had forgotten. The loss of a separate sense of self, a solid self-image, appears to lift the lid that has hidden from view all the qualities and feelings that were considered uncomfortable or unacceptable. In Western psychology, this lid is known as the "repression barrier," and the early stages of embodiment often involve facing and ultimately embracing this previously repressed material. During this phase, which can be both daunting and disconcerting, students often complain that awakening has left them feeling worse rather than better.

Eventually, through the process of embodiment described in the first part of this chapter, most of these emotions are welcomed and embraced, and there's an ongoing ease in facing whatever else arises and letting it be, without resistance or struggle. But the core patterns, the deeper roots, tend to persist, often because they exist not beneath the level of conscious awareness, as repressed emotions do, but in a separate domain, like little selves whose emptiness has not yet been revealed. One particularly clear and awakened friend of mine experienced herself as the limitless vastness of being and seemed to live in constant joy—until she was suddenly ambushed by the return of old fears. Eventually, she began recovering memories of being molested by her father, along with the inner sense of a separate part of herself that was still terrified and alone.

From a Western psychological perspective, these separate parts are often the result of dissociation, the splitting of the self into parts, rather than the repression of certain aspects of the self into the unconscious. At some particularly stressful point in a person's life history, a part of the self walls itself off to protect itself from what it perceives to be a life-threatening situation. This maneuver may help the psyche survive an abusive or otherwise traumatic childhood, but later the splits may prove difficult to acknowledge and heal.

Because these parts don't simply rise to awareness once the self-image has shattered, they remain hidden from view and may need to be actively invited and approached. Otherwise, they continue to engage in emotional hijacking, putting forth intense emotions—seemingly from nowhere—that lead to unexpected bouts of contraction and reactivity. Sometimes these parts exert their influence primarily through mysterious physical problems such as chronic pain, digestive problems, or autoimmune disorders. People dealing with these unacknowledged parts may feel quite awakened, spacious, and free in most of their being most of the time but have pockets of dissociation and fixation that have never seen the light and are still seething with unexpressed emotion. Buddhist psychologist Edward Podvoll called these dissociated parts "islands of insanity," where we may run aground from time to time as we sail through the ocean of the Self.

From the perspective of brain research, these deeply rooted patterns or dissociated parts are hardwired into the "old brain," particularly the amygdala, which processes and stores memories associated with emotional events. Instinc-

Breathe and Reflect

Spend some time considering the ways in which emotional hijacking occurs in your own life. How do your actions not quite live up to your level of spiritual understanding? What kinds of circumstances are particularly disturbing for you? How do you deal with your demons, those sudden, unexpected outbursts of contraction and pain?

tive or emotional reactions that originate in the old brain often bypass the information and wisdom that the "new brain," or neocortex, has accumulated over a lifetime of experience and thought. As a result, you can live in the timeless spiritual dimension of being from your neocortex, which is the seat of "higher consciousness," but still be fearful about your future survival or enraged about unresolved past traumas in your old-brain emotional centers.

Whatever metaphor you choose, psychological or neurological, the message is still the same: despite powerful awakening experiences, you may still have profound internal splits that perpetuate division and conflict at a psychological level and lead to actions that are out of harmony or integrity with the nondual reality to which you've awakened. Until every split has fully healed and you experience no separation between outside and inside, self and other—and one part of yourself and another—your realization hasn't completely embodied.

Healing the Split

My Advaita teacher Jean Klein, who was trained as a medical doctor, used to say that the key to healing was to "invade the unhealthy part with the healthy part"—in other words, infuse the unawakened, unhealed parts of the being with the spaciousness and love of consciousness, or true nature. At retreats, he would have us focus on the parts of our body that felt healthy and light and imagine them penetrating the parts that felt constricted and dense. Such deliberate techniques are often necessary for deepening the process of embodiment to the split-off parts of the being. In the words of Adyashanti, we need to "close the gap."

One way to close the gap is to invite a part to express itself fully by giving voice to its feelings and concerns while you not only listen empathically, but also allow yourself to experience what this part must be experiencing from the inside. (Psychological techniques that employ this approach include voice dialogue, inner-child work, and ego-state psychology.) Here again, compassionate awareness and a genuine willingness to enter the reality of the dissociated part—that is, a willingness to put your head in the demon's mouth—is the key to healing the split. Another approach is to abide as the spacious wakefulness of your true nature and imagine breathing in the suffering of the contracted, unhealed part and breathing out peace, love, and ease of being. (This variation on the Tibetan practice of *tonglen* is described more fully at the end of this chapter.) Still another approach is the therapeutic technique known as somatic experiencing, which invites participants to gradually heal the "trauma vortex" (the split-off part or core of fixated energy) by accessing the positive, nourishing inner resources of the "healing vortex" and gently "pendulating" between the two. Finally, there's the modality called eye movement desensitization and reprocessing (EMDR), which uses bilateral (left-right) stimulation to fully process and digest unresolved traumas and the splits they create.

As it turns out, many of these healing techniques require the active involvement of a helping professional. Because the painful inner splits generally occurred as the result of traumatic or unwholesome relationships, they tend to be healed most successfully in the context of another relationship—one that's loving rather than abusive, reparative rather than damaging. The nondual spiritual traditions almost exclusively emphasize individual practice and realization and fail to recognize the importance of healing relationships. But increasingly, these traditions are appreciating the value of the relational model encouraged by Western psychology.

However you work to heal the split, it's important to remember that the challenging reactive patterns and core stories have nothing to do with who you really are, which is pure, unconditioned consciousness or wakefulness. Your true nature is undisturbed and indestructible; no experience can ever stain or damage it, and it never stops being who you are, no matter how much you suffer.

By all means, face and embrace the troublesome samskaras and take responsibility for their impact on your life, but don't mistake them for who you are or blame or judge yourself as inadequate because you still have them, even though you've awakened. Self-judgment is just another of ego's little ploys to reestablish its power. Who knows where these samskaras come from? Genetics? Past lives? Astrological influences? Family constellations? And who knows whether they will ever fully release their hold, no matter how many awakenings you have or how earnestly you aspire to embody? Wherever they originate and however they evolve, remember that they're not personal (as if anything could be); they're just karmic bundles you're handed in this lifetime in a most impersonal way and asked to carry and ultimately unwrap.

In the end, embodiment is always both endless and instantaneous. From the absolute perspective, every moment and situation is the perfect embodiment or manifestation of the Divine. Nothing is ever amiss and everything is as it should be, because this timeless moment is all there is. At the same time, until you actually experience everything and every situation as your very own self and act accordingly, you're still engaged in the ongoing process of embodying. Here again, you encounter the paradox of the gateless gate, but at a deeper level: you're already inherently embodied, but until your every action reflects the realization of divine perfection, you haven't fully actualized this embodiment. As the sacred symbol of the cross implies, the timeless vertical dimension (pure being, innate perfection) and the horizontal dimension (endless evolution and becoming) meet right here in the eternal Now.

Your account of the misguided roshi who had received so many Dharma transmissions makes me wonder about the legitimacy of traditional lineages. Is there any point in perpetuating the institution of gurus and roshis and the spiritual hierarchies that support them?

I prefer the notion of the "spiritual friend" (a translation of the Buddhist term *kalyana mitra*), someone who helps guide

you on your journey but doesn't participate in spiritual hierarchies or pretend to be someone or something you're not.
Personally, I feel deep gratitude for the teachers I've had,
especially those who awakened out of traditional frameworks and taught in original and unconventional ways. Not
only did their freedom from limitation galvanize my own
realization, but they were so accessible, so undefended—
defining characteristics of truly awakened human beings.

**You seem to be suggest that psychotherapy
can be helpful in some cases to assist in the
process of deeper embodiment. What
should I look for in a therapist?**

Once you've awakened to who you really are, you may
understandably be suspicious of conventional psychotherapy because it can tend to reinforce the drama of the illusory
separate self. At the same time, as long as you continue to be
"hijacked" by old reactive patterns, certain forms of therapy
may prove helpful in healing the split. For short-term trauma
work, you might do well with a skilled, empathic therapist in
your area who's experienced in the practice of somatic experiencing or EMDR. For ongoing support in exploring the
core stories and stuck places that have become especially
apparent in the aftermath of awakening, I recommend someone in the emerging field of nondual psychotherapy. These
practitioners have studied the nondual teachings, experienced some level of awakening themselves, and now incor-

porate their realization in their work with others. Instead of seeing you as damaged and in need of repair, therapists with a nondual perspective see beyond the personality to your inherent perfection and support you in living from the truth of who you are; at the same time, they help you to recognize and explore the stories, beliefs, and emotional patterns that cause you suffering. For more information on the growing influence of nondual wisdom on psychotherapy, consult the anthology *The Sacred Mirror* (cited in the bibliography at the end of this book). (For information on the nondual therapy and spiritual counseling I offer by phone, visit my website at stephanbodian.org.)

Wake-Up Call

Embracing Your Demons

Set aside fifteen to twenty minutes for this exploration. Begin by sitting quietly with your eyes closed for a few minutes. Rest your awareness on the experience of sitting, and allow your body to relax.

Now connect with the limitless peace, spaciousness, and love of your essential nature, your true self. If you find this difficult, connect with the place in your heart where you feel unconditional love. Allow this feeling of peace, spaciousness, and love to expand infinitely in every direction.

Next, imagine that your small self, the little me who struggles and suffers, is in front of you. Alternatively, you may want to focus on a particularly troubled or conflicted part of yourself, a part that keeps demanding your attention by repeatedly generating fear, anger, grief, or other constrictive emotions. Let yourself visualize and empathize with this little me.

Imagine yourself breathing in the suffering of your small self and breathing out peace, love, joy, and forgiveness. Allow this love and joy to fill the small self and heal its suffering. Continue to breathe in the suffering and breathe out the love and joy until you've absorbed the suffering of the small self back into the vastness of your true self. The apparent gap has dissolved, and peace, love, and joy are all-pervasive.

Even though this exercise may seem dualistic or contrived, it can have a powerful healing effect on the parts of you that may not feel so spiritually awakened or attuned. You're embodying the truth you know yourself to be and healing the internal split between conscious and unconscious, awake and asleep. Embodiment is not complete until every part has been embraced and included.

10

THE AWAKENED LIFE

All you have to do is find out your source and take up
your headquarters there.

—*Nisargadatta Maharaj*

*W*hen you act from the recognition that everyone
and everything without exception is the divine expression,
consciousness in manifestation, spirit incarnate, you're living
the awakened life. Wherever you look, you see nothing but
your very own Self. You're both the limitless openness in
which everything arises and at the same time every part and
particle of what is. All sense of separation has dissolved, and
there's just this single living, breathing reality.

Although this experience of no-separation is often
called "oneness," it doesn't mean that you've lost the everyday sense of being an individual person and merged into
some undifferentiated mass in which all distinctions have
disappeared, as many people mistakenly believe. Quite the
contrary, everyone and everything is crystal clear in its
radiant uniqueness, yet you simultaneously recognize that
this uniqueness and diversity is just the creative play and

expression of the Self, which is the single source and essence of all.

When you see everything as the divine expression, including what you once took to belong to you—your body, your thoughts, your feelings—you move with the flow of life instead of struggling against the current. Even saying "you move" is extra because there's no separate you to do the moving or deciding, just the flow of life itself that moves through you, as it moves through the rock, the bird, the river, the tree.

In practical terms, you're no longer arguing or bargaining with life in an attempt to get it to be different from the way it is, because you know it can't be otherwise. "Not my will, but Thy will be done" is the mantra of the awakened life. Indeed, your will is no longer different from God's because you've completely surrendered to what is just the way it is. Even words like *surrendered* make no sense—there's simply no separation.

Needless to say, the awakened life is marked by ease, peace, joy, equanimity, and above all, love. Since everything is your very own Self, your radiant consciousness, your innate Buddha nature, you're thoroughly intimate and in love with everyone and everything you encounter. In the limitless emptiness once inhabited by a self-image, the richness and indescribable beauty of reality blossoms, and you're endlessly open, fascinated, moved, and delighted with how this reality is expressing itself right now. To put it another way, consciousness is delighting in itself in all its forms through this particular body and mind. Relationships take on an extraordinary immediacy when you know that every person you meet is merely you in a different disguise. Hope and fear drop away as you realize that the illusory separate self has no control anyway, and everything is held in God's tender embrace.

Not that life always works out the way the mind may want it to, now that you know who you are. This isn't the New Age or the "best of all possible worlds" of Voltaire's *Candide*. No, life unfolds exactly the way it does, in its own mysterious, at times intense and incomprehensible, yet strangely balanced and meaningful way, and you find yourself wanting it to be exactly the way it is. Ups and downs, successes and failures, health and illness—the river flows endlessly on, constantly changing, constantly in motion, while the unmoved mover, the source of all, is ever undisturbed and untouched by what occurs.

At the same time, you may continue to live a very ordinary life, with the same tastes, preferences, and personality quirks as before. The difference is that you no longer mistakenly identify with the personality, but instead recognize it as just a convenient vehicle or role through which the Self expresses itself in the world of manifestation. (The root of the word *personality* literally means to "sound through" and refers to the masks worn by the chorus in Greek tragedy.) Now that you recognize the inherently empty nature of reality, you no longer take your "personal" life quite so seriously. You both care and don't care, you're in the world but not of it, and you greet every situation with a certain lightness and bemusement because you know it's just the mysterious play of the Divine.

The more fully and deeply you embody the truth of who you are, the more consistently you live the awakened life from moment to moment. In this sense, complete embodiment is identical with the stabilization of the awakened experience. You see nothing but God or Buddha everywhere you look, 24-7, and your actions reflect this nondual vision. Some sages call this fully stabilized and unbroken experience of no-self/no-other "liberation" to distinguish it from mere "awakening." Once you're liberated, you can't possibly treat others in insensitive, abusive, or self-serving ways, as some purportedly enlightened teachers do, because you can't help but see them as your very own Self.

Just because you've awakened doesn't mean you're always living the awakened life, however. Most people live the awakened life episodically, for hours, days, perhaps weeks at a time before they once again become enthralled by the illusion of a separate self. This reidentification may be ever so subtle and go unnoticed unless there's a deep commitment to the transformative fire of truth, but it has enormous ramifications. In particular, once you take yourself for a separate someone again, you start seeing the world from a self-centered perspective and falling under the trance of the old reactive patterns and core stories that used to run your life. For the awakened life to continue to live itself through you, you need to be dedicated to allowing the embodiment process (described in the previous two chapters) and to actualizing the truth you know yourself to be in every situation.

HOW THE AWAKENED LIFE LOOKS FROM THE OUTSIDE

The term *awakened life* tends to conjure images of cloistered monks, wandering yogis, and spiritual teachers bestowing the truth on their devoted disciples. But those who embody the peace and joy of the awakened heart may just as readily be ordinary folks you meet on the street—the garbage collector, the housecleaner, the bank teller, the healer. That is, folks like you and me. Not everyone who discovers and lives from the light of his or her true self feels moved to teach or retreat from the world. Some just wake up spontaneously and go on living the same life as before—doing their job, taking care of their family, watching TV, going to the movies—with the significant difference that they no longer suffer or struggle with life and no longer experience themselves as separate from others.

Those who live the awakened life don't generally draw attention to themselves with extravagant acts of compas-

Breathe and Reflect

Close your eyes and imagine yourself living the awakened life. How does it feel to go about your day seeing everyone and everything you meet as your very own Self? How do you act when you're merged with the flow of life instead of resisting it? Spend a few minutes allowing this visualization to unfold. How does it affect your experience of life when you open your eyes again?

sion or self-conscious words of wisdom. Instead, they tend to fade into the background because they're so ordinary, so down-to-earth, so unobtrusive, so empty of themselves. If they do teach, they have no attachment to the role and status of teacher. As a young Zen monk, I visited a nearby Buddhist center to catch a glimpse of the great Tibetan yogi Kalu Rinpoche and found a half-dozen monks sitting around a table eating lunch. From their behavior, the way they ate and talked and interacted, I couldn't tell the rinpoche from the others until someone pointed him out. I was deeply impressed that this illustrious master didn't exhibit the slightest trace of pride or pretension. This ordinariness, I realized, is the true mark of the awakened life.

If you peer beneath the apparent ordinariness, however, you'll find that, regardless of personality or life situation, those who embody the awakened life have certain qualities in common. For example, they tend to exude a peaceful, imperturbable presence, and their eyes tend to radiate a sense of infinite spaciousness and compassion, which reveals that there's no one there looking, just consciousness or spirit gazing at itself. In action, they tend to move smoothly and harmoniously through life without internal conflict or division, quietly joyful, unobtrusively kind and empathetic, yet subtly disengaged and free of concern. Of course, these qualities can express themselves through an infinite spectrum of bodies, voices, and personalities. Some may be animated and energetic, others more quiet and introspective.

Even enlightened teachers and sages come in a wide variety of shapes and dispositions. The great Indian sage

Ramana Maharshi spent most of his days and nights sitting or lying in placid repose wearing only a loincloth, teaching largely through silent gazing or brief answers to his devotees, and taking daily walks up the holy mountain on which his ashram was situated. His eyes were the embodiment of the peace and love of the Self. By contrast, the renowned Advaita teacher Nisargadatta Maharaj ran a small cigarette shop by day and gave talks and answered questions from the seekers who gathered in his little apartment in Bombay at night. As he spoke, his eyes blazed with intensity, his hands gesticulated wildly, and his voice occasionally grew loud in his passion for truth.

My Advaita teacher, Jean Klein, was a cultured European gentleman who wore silk shirts and cravats and enjoyed good food, great art, and classical music. His public dialogues were generally punctuated by long silences between the words, and his teachings, delivered in a soft but deeply resonant voice, were articulate, powerful, and to the point. By contrast, my friend and teacher Adyashanti is a California native who used to race bicycles and climb rocks and now enjoys a good poker game and motorcycle rides in the country. His satsangs have a more casual, contemporary feel and are punctuated as often by laughter as by silence. Yet the truth they convey is identical to the truth conveyed by his predecessors.

In the end, the only conclusion we can make about the awakened life is that it assumes the form and personality of the person who lives it. You can't imitate it or will it to happen; you can only wake up, live the truth of your awakening, and notice how life lives through you. The awakened life is the ultimate fruition and expression of the process that begins with your initial awakening. As I said at the start of this chapter, when you act from the recognition that everything without exception is the divine expression, consciousness in manifestation, spirit incarnate, you're living the awakened life.

Wake-Up Call

Let It All Go

Set aside ten minutes for this exploration. Spend a few minutes sitting quietly and enjoying your breath. Now reflect on your experience of reading this book, and consider all the beliefs and concepts about spiritual awakening you may have accumulated along the way. Perhaps you have a more clearly developed and articulated picture of how the process of awakening unfolds. Or perhaps you've just collected a few assorted insights and ideas.

Next, relax the fixation of energy in the brain and imagine all the ideas and concepts dissolving into emptiness, like ice dissolving into water. Don't hold on to anything. Let it all go. Whatever you need, you already have, so set down your baggage and allow the river of life to take you.

Rest in the limitless spaciousness and emptiness of innocent looking, don't-know mind. Remember that reality begins and ends right here, in this timeless moment. Nothing else is needed, and nothing is left out. You already are what you seek. Just be it!

OTHER BOOKS
YOU MIGHT ENJOY

Adams, Robert. *Silence of the Heart*. Atlanta, Ga.: Acropolis Books, 1999.

Adyashanti. *Emptiness Dancing*. Boulder, Colo.: Sounds True, 2005.

Carse, David. *Perfect Brilliant Stillness: Beyond the Individual Self*. Shelburne, Vt.: Paragate Publishing, 2006.

Harding, Douglas. *On Having No Head: Zen and the Rediscovery of the Obvious*. Carlsbad, Calif.: Inner Directions, 2002.

Katie, Byron. *A Thousand Names for Joy: Living in Harmony with the Way Things Are*. New York City: Harmony Books, 2007.

Khenpo, Nyoshul. *Natural Great Perfection*. Ithaca, N.Y.: Snow Lion, 1995.

Klein, Jean. *Who Am I?* Salisbury, UK: Non-Duality Press, 2006.

Maharaj, Nisargadatta. *Ultimate Medicine: Dialogues with a Realized Master*. Berkeley, Calif.: North Atlantic Books, 2006.

Maharshi, Ramana. *Be As You Are: The Teachings of Sri Ramana Maharshi*. New York City: Penguin, 1989.

Parsons, Tony. *As It Is: The Open Secret to Living an Awakened Life*. Carlsbad, Calif.: Inner Directions, 2000.

Prendergast, John, Peter Fenner, and Sheila Krystal, eds. *The Sacred Mirror: Nondual Wisdom and Psychotherapy*. St. Paul, Minn.: Paragon House, 2003.

Segal, Suzanne. *Collision with the Infinite.* Delhi, India: Motilal
    Banarsidass, 2002.

Tolle, Eckhart. *The Power of Now: A Guide to Spiritual
    Enlightenment.* Novato, Calif.: New World Library, 1997.

INDEX

ABOUT THE AUTHOR

$\mathcal{S}$tephan Bodian, founder and director of the School for Awakening, has been teaching the direct approach to spiritual awakening for more than thirty years. Currently his life is devoted to igniting and fostering the flame of truth in others through his counseling, mentoring, teaching, and writing. Ordained a Zen monk in 1974, Stephan studied with some of the great spiritual masters of our age. After a series of deepening awakenings, he received Dharma transmission from Adyashanti.

The former editor-in-chief of *Yoga Journal*, Stephan is the author of the bestselling guidebook *Meditation for Dummies* and coauthor of *Buddhism for Dummies*. A psychotherapist as well as a spiritual teacher, he has been a pioneer in the integration of the timeless spiritual wisdom of the East and the insights of Western psychology. For more information about the eight-month School for Awakening or about intensives, retreats, or spiritual counseling by phone, visit his website at **stephanbodian.org**.